George Bernard Shaw's

Historical Plays

George Bernard Shaw's

Historical Plays

R. N. Roy, Reader
Post-graduate Department of English
Nagpur University

SBN: 33390 130 4

M

First published, 1976, by
THE MACMILLAN COMPANY OF INDIA LIMITED
Delhi   Bombay   Calcutta   Madras
Associated companies throughout the world

ISBN 0 333 21970 8

Published by S G Wasani for The Macmillan Company
of India Limited and printed at Prabhat Press, Meerut.

To
Geoffrey Bullough
With grateful regards

Contents

Contents

Preface

George Bernard Shaw wrote four plays on historical themes—*The Man of Destiny, Caesar and Cleopatra, Saint Joan* and *In Good King Charles's Golden Days.* Though they form a substantial part of his dramatic output, their sources and their historical veracity, Shaw's historical method and his notion of historical truth have not yet been sufficiently investigated. Nor could I investigate them in my doctoral dissertation *George Bernard Shaw's Philosophy of Life*. This is my apology for writing one more book on Shaw.

Shaw was a gigantic figure who bestrode 'modern thought like a colossus', but he was not a historian. He was an ardent Creative Evolutionist and he exploited history to champion the cause of Creative Evolution. However, the success of his historical plays shows what he could have achieved if he had devoted himself to historical drama. *The Man of Destiny* is a small piece of quality that displays, to use Shaw's own words, 'my knowledge of stage tricks'. *Caesar and Cleopatra* is one of the most remarkable modern historical plays; *In Good King Charles's Golden Days* is a *tour de force*; and *Saint Joan* is, in many respects, the best work of literary art on that most baffling theme, and, perhaps, the greatest historical drama since Shakespeare. It provide sa consistent picture of the Maid of France who has baffled the wits of writers for five centuries, and more as also a provocative interpretation of the trial that is 'second in importance only to the trial of Christ'. Shaw's *Saint Joan* is 'as greatly praised by historians as by dramatic critics'.

The main purpose of the present study is an examination of the content and not the form of Shaw's historical plays, though I have also devoted some space to the examination of their literary and theatrical qualities; for, although for an understanding of Shaw and his wide influence it is necessary to have a clear notion of his thought and philosophy, he is essentially a playwright.

In preparing this book I had the proud privilege of getting the guidance of two eminent critics—Professor Geoffrey Bullough and Professor S.C. Sengupta. From them I have learnt more than I can hope to acknowledge. I am deeply in debt to Hon. Mr. M. Hidyatullah, Chief Justice of India, and Dr. L. Raymond, His Grace the Lord Archbishop of Nagpur, who took the trouble to read through the manuscript and suggest improvements in those sections where I trench on legal and judicial and religious matters.

I encountered considerable difficulty in completing the chapter on *Saint Joan*, for the records of the two trials and most of the book son Joan are not available in India. I am grateful to Professor Y. M. Muley, Librarian, Nagpur University, who procured the records and the books I needed from the National Central Library, London; the Library of Congress, Washington; the Commonwealth National Library, Australia; the Library of New South Wales, Sydney; the Government of India National Library, Calcutta; and the Bombay University Library, Bombay.

In the references I have tried to acknowledge my debt to the various writers I have drawn on, and I wish to offer my sincere apologies if, through inadvertence, I have used any matter without due acknowledgement.

Nagpur   R. N. ROY
26 March 1976

1. Introduction

Bernard Shaw wrote on a variety of subjects, but the most dominant theme in his dramatic works is the evolution of the race. After making a moral and intellectual analysis of contemporary civilisation, he was convinced that man as a species had made little progress and that he was doomed if he persisted in his present inadequacy. Man must ever evolve into a higher and higher being if he is not to be scrapped. Out of a deep sense of human failure Shaw became a Creative Evolutionist, glorifying the mystic urge for betterment. It is this basic idea which inspires his social criticism and the dramas in which the doctrine of the Life Force does not come to the forefront.

The idea of Creative Evolution is not one that Shaw vamped up for *Man and Superman* and *Back to Methuselah* only; it pervades all his work. Shaw's mind had been unconsciously engaged upon Creative Evolution from the very beginning of his literary career. For him the central reality is the Life Force, and his faith in Vitalism is evident in his early writings. His Vitalism made him search for heroic characters, for it is through great men that he entertained hope for humanity. Great men prove that it is possible for man to rise to a higher position in the scale of evolution than that which average humanity has attained. They are the harbingers of what man one day may become. In the Preface to *Geneva* Shaw says, 'The apparent freaks of nature called Great Men mark not human attainment but human possibility and hope. They prove that though we in the mass are only child Yahoos it is possible for creatures built exactly like us, bred from our unions and developed from our seeds, to reach the heights of these towering heads.'[1] Great men gave Shaw a deep and satisfying faith in a brighter future for man. Shaw, like Carlyle, combines deep faith in great men with contempt for the people. His faith in great men as humanity's only hope as well as his contempt for the rabble is demonstrated even in his early writings,[2] and this attitude is not a sporadic but a permanent characteristic of his mind. Great men gave him something to look forward to, something to hope for.

With this deep faith in great men, Shaw attempted in his works to create superior individuals. Edward Conolly, Owen Jack,

Cashel Byron, Bluntschli, Eugene Marchbanks are early but incomplete attempts and partial forecasts of the Superman of Shaw's idea. Though they possess some degree of immunity from the weaknesses and passions which ordinary human beings are liable to, none of them comes up to Shaw's conception of a great man. Shaw must have realised this fact, and he turned to history for great men in whom life had expressed itself at a comparatively high level. And it is in the sketches of historical heroes, in Caesar (1898) and in a lesser degree in Napoleon (1896), that we find the first concrete applications of the tenets of Shaw's philosophy of Creative Evolution.

II

Shaw is primarily a Creative Evolutionist and his views on other subjects—economics, politics, history, etc., are subsidiary to his advocacy of the cause of Creative Evolution. An ardent believer in Creative Evolution, he regards everybody as an experiment of the Life Force and looks into history for great men to be dramatised from this point of view. His purpose is to set examples of great historical individuals, like Napoleon, Caesar, Saint Joan, whose evolutionary qualities posterity might admire and imitate. In each of his historical plays Shaw has kept his attention riveted on a great individual, an individual of central historical significance. His purpose is to bring out the heroic qualities of the individual and he often brings them out quite successfully. But he often tailors his hero to his own particular view of greatness, and hence a clear conception of his view of greatness is a prerequisite for a clear understanding of his historical plays.

A Shavian great man is a man of originality and this originality gives him 'an air of frankness, generosity, and magnanimity by enabling him to estimate the value of truth, money or success in any particular instance quite independently of convention and moral generalisation'.[3] He is a realist in that he is free from romantic illusion and sees things exactly as they are. A great experiment of the Life Force, a great man has, above all, an indomitable will, which can be identified with what he conceives to be the purpose of the world or of God. He has his eyes fixed on his goal from which he will never swerve and for which all causes must give way. To reach his goal he will act with entire selfishness, tell dexterous lies and stoop to any kind of subterfuge. All these qualities endow a great man with rare personality and power which all around him feel. He can, therefore, manipulate things and beings to his own purpose. But his intellect is never beglamoured or his aim shaken by a sense of his own power or by any other passion, particularly never by love of women (of whom he may be fond but who can never deflect him from his chosen path). He is conscious of a great purpose and he possesses the will to act upon it. This high degree of will accounts for his tremendous control over himself. A Shavian great man is not free from fear, and he is without courage which is a prime virtue of Carlyle's and Nietzsche's heroes. But he wills his ends so strongly that even the one universal passion, fear, finds no place in him. And though without courage, his mind is so firmly fixed on his goal that he ignores all dangers. Thus he flies in the face of danger not because he possesses courage in the sense of a disposition to defy danger but because he is oblivious of it. Shaw's Napoleon, for example, knows 'fear well, better than you, better than any woman', but once on the bridge at Lodi it cannot hold him back. Oblivious of fear, a great man is also oblivious of courage. As Eric Bentley says, 'If Nietzsche's hero is beyond good and evil, Shaw's is beyond courage and cowardice.'[4]

A great man triumphs over his environment and achieves his goal by virtue of his intelligence and shrewdness, but more by his unconventional attitude and steady will power. He is not the creature of his age but its creator, not its servant but its master. He controls events and drives society in the direction which he wishes it to go. This is a genius which means clear sightedness, will and ability to influence other people. This conception of the great man brings Shaw into sharp conflict with the scientific view of history. A scientific historian seeks to explain all changes in thought, all movements in politics and society in terms of unswerving natural laws. The individual, according to this view, is immersed in and driven by the current of social tendencies. The scientific historian looks upon social life as an organism unfolding itself according to immanent laws; either of racial individuality or of a combination of social, physical and personal forces. The spirit of a people and of an age outweighs the power of an individual's personality which can work only along socially conditioned tendencies. The habit of a scientific historian is thus to subordinate, if not quite eliminate, the individual; the greatest man is treated by him as in a large measure the product and expression of the spirit of the time. For Shaw, on the contrary, the great man is supreme. External circumstances and influences count little. According to him, the great man surmounts the environmental forces, and it is his personal initiative that accounts for history.

Shaw's conception of history is the very opposite of deterministic. The determinists hold that history is the record of a constant process of evolution towards a predetermined goal in which a great man plays only a very limited part while Shaw regards the course of history as flexible and open to salutary modification by the well instructed human will. Nothing that happens is inevitable, because man has the power to control his own destiny. The idea of human will looms large in Shaw's conception of history.

Anti-scientific in his reading of history, Shaw is also anti-democraticin the lesson he deduces from it. Each of his historical plays is the product of a great mind in opposition to the rabble. Shaw laments that there has been no progress during the last 2500 years, but he believes in the possibility of progress. History gives glimpses of progress followed by decadent civilisations. Occasional progress has been possible only because of superior individuals who had the greatness to bring order out of chaos and turn decadence to discipline. But great men are rare, and hence there has been no continuity of progress. This idea is implicit in Shaw's historical plays. The lesson that can be derived from these plays is that the one hope of the distracted world lies in the strength and wisdom of the few, not in the organised unwisdom of the many. The masses of people can never solve for themselves the intricate problems of their own welfare. They need to be guided, disciplined, at times even driven, by those great leaders of men who know much better than they can ever know what is good for them, and how that good is to be attained. In the Preface to *Back to Methuselah* Shaw wrote in 1920 of 'a doubt which had grown steadily in my mind during my forty years public work as a Socialist: namely, whether the human animal, as he exists at present, is capable of solving the social problems raised by his own aggregation or, as he calls it, his civilization'.[5] And earlier, in 1901, in *The Revolutionist's Handbook* he had already reiterated the need for the Superman. Shaw, like Carlyle, is anti-scientific and anti-democratic in his study of history.

III

Shaw's historical plays are direct descendants of the nineteenth century historical drama in that each one of them exploits at least two, if not all the three, characteristics of that genre—elaborate spectacle, erotic intrigue and flamboyant histrionics. As a dramatic critic he had become well acquainted with all the popular tricks of the trade, and he exploited and adopted most of them with virtuosity. He often turned to his predecessors in the field and followed their technique. He says:

> Technically, I do not find myself able to proceed otherwise than as former playwrights have done. True, my plays have the latest mechanical improvements: the action is not carried on by impossible soliloquies and asides; and my people get on and off the stage without requiring four doors to a room which in real life would have only one. But my stories are the old stories; my characters are the familiar harlequin and columbine, clown and pantaloon (note the harlequin's leap in the third act of Caesar and Cleopatra); my stage tricks and suspenses and thrills and the jests are the ones in vogue when I was a boy, by which time my grandfather was tired of them.[6]

The Man of Destiny exploits the erotic intrigue and flamboyant histrionics of the nineteenth century history play. Caesar and Cleopatra exploits the elaborate spectacle and flamboyant histrionics, and though it is one of the three plays for Puritans that attempt to be anti-erotic yet here 'the consummation of romantic love is suggested. Mark Antony, who never sets foot on the stage, hovers on the edges of the play; the future spells the assassination of Caesar and the romance of Antony.'[7] Saint Joan exploits the elaborate spectacle and the histrionics, and In Good King Charles's Golden Days exploits significantly the erotic aspect. Shaw did not entirely break away from the nineteenth century history play, but 'turned for guidance to the dramatists who were his immediate predecessors and laid a heavy toll on them'.[8]

Shaw, however, differs from the nineteenth century historical drama in this fundamental respect that he often gives the immediacy and familiarity of the present to the past.　He set forth Caesar in the same modern light, taking the platform from Shakespeare, with no thought of pretending to express Mommsenite view of Caesar any more than Shakespeare set out to express a Plutarchian view.　In the Preface to *Saint Joan* he flatly declares that in order to make a twentieth-century audience conscious of an epoch fundamentally different from its own he had to endow the medieval characters with twentieth-century consciousness:

> But it is the business of the stage to make its figures more intelligible to themselves than they could be in real life; for by no other means can they be made intelligible to the audience. And in this case Cauchon and Lemaiter have to make intelligible not only themselves but the Church and the Inquisition, just as Warwick has to make the feudal system intelligible, the three between them having thus to make a twentieth-century audience conscious of an epoch fundamentally different from its own. Obviously the real Cauchon, Lemaiter, and Warwick could not have done this: they were part of the Middle Ages themselves, and therefore as unconscious of its peculiarities as of the atomic formula of the air they breathed. But the play would be unintelligible if I had not endowed them with enough of this consciousness to enable them to explain their attitude to the twentieth century. All I claim is that by this inevitable sacrifice of verisimilitude I have secured in the only possible way sufficient veracity to justify me in claiming that as far as I can gather from the available documentation, and from such powers of divination as I possess, the things I represent these three exponents of the drama as saying are the things they actually would have said if they had known what they were really doing. And beyond this neither drama nor history can go in my hands.[9]

Shaw admittedly portrays historical characters on the basis of modern analogies, rubbing off as much as possible the patina of time from them.　Apollodorus's declaration that his 'motto is Art for Art's Sake', Ftatateeta's complaint that Cleopatra wants to be 'what these Romans call a New Woman' jolt the audience from the ancient to the modern world.　The remote and unfamiliar world of the nineteenth century historical drama stands as a contrast to Shaw's world where contemporaneity breaks through again and again.

Let us pause here for a moment to indicate whether Shaw's method of interpreting history by the application of present-day attitudes and modes of expression to medieval or ancient situations and characters is historical. Historical facts are always refracted through the mind of the historian, and personal temperament, experience, conviction and the environment of the time and place are the determinants of historical truth. It has been aptly said that 'there are no final value-judgments of time or history, but always new judgments, reflecting new conditions surrounding those who do the judging'.[10] The facts of history 'do not and cannot exist in a pure form'. As E.H. Carr says, 'New vistas, new angles of vision, constantly appear as the procession—and the historian with it—moves along. The historian is part of history. The point in the procession at which he finds himself determines his angle of vision over the past. This truism is not less true when the period treated by the historian is remote from his own time.'[11] Carl G. Gustavson is more explicit and more emphatic: 'A historian cannot avoid portraying history according to his personal valuation of it, and also, if he would be understood by his contemporaries, he must clothe his thoughts in the distinctive mood of expression of his own age.'[12] No doubt facts and documents are essential to the historian, but they do not themselves constitute history, and hence 'do not make fetish of them'.[13] Nowadays 'we are less obsessed by the demand for critical accuracy and more interested in interpreting facts'.[14] Indeed, 'the history we read, though based on fact is, strictly speaking, not factual at all, but a series of accepted judgments.'[15] All that clearly emerges is that the belief in a hard core of historical facts existing objectively and independently of the interpretation of the historian is erroneous. The historian is constantly moulding his facts to his interpretation, and the thought of the historian is always moulded by the environment of the time and place. Indeed, as Engels says, 'A system of natural and historical knowledge which is all embracing and final for all time is in contradiction to the fundamental laws of dialectical thinking.'[16] As every author reflects in his work his own opinions and the opinions of his age, Shaw's interpretation of historical events and persons in his own personal way and his presentation of them in the light of his own time are not unhistorical.

It must also be pointed out here that Shaw has great faith in his own theories and he approaches history with pre-conceived notions, biases and preferences. But all this does not matter. For, every historian has his 'sets of presuppositions', 'sets of preconceptions'.[17] Indeed, 'no historian approaches his task without certain preconceived and systematic generalisations about the course of the human past.'[18]

Shaw also does not take into account the fact that each age has its own peculiarities and that individuals are ruled by a complicated and ever-shifting fabric of custom, law, society and politics, events at home and abroad. He does not place a historical figure in the centre of actual historical forces and show how his actions were determined partly by his environment and partly by his character. He often places him in an imaginary situation instead, like the encounter between the Man of Destiny and the Strange Lady, and deals with certain fundamental traits of human character which the historical figure shares in common with himself. He says, 'As a dramatist, I have no clue to any historical or other personage save that part of him which is also myself.'[19] Sometimes he infuses into the historical character something of himself, or invests him with certain superman-like qualities even though he may not possess them. Charles II's views on education, the English race and on how to choose rulers are the views of Shaw himself, and Caesar's complete immunity from passion of vengeance and his complete indifference to the call of sex when there is serious work to be done are superman-like qualities which the Caesar of history did not possess.

Shaw thus took many liberties with history. But that is immaterial. Shakespeare too, as Professor Geoffrey Bullough says, 'departed from the full facts in small things and in large, in his English and Roman plays, yet gave an overall view of events and people which we accept because it is consistent with itself and vital, and is what we would expect an Elizabethan writer to make of the periods concerned'.[20] What is material from our point of view is that in using historical people and facts, and in giving a view of them essentially of his own time, affected by his Creative Evolution ideas and by Nietzsche and Schopenhauer, Shaw made four plays which are laudable works of art. Shaw is a dramatist, and in these plays he has given us his considered opinion on the people and the periods concerned from the twentieth century viewpoint, and that is what we would expect a modern writer to do.

Historians, especially historians of the scientific school, whose yardstick is truth to historical fact and historical probability, may find fault with Shaw's delineation of historical figures. But they are not the only persons to judge whether historical figures are well drawn by writers of fiction. The fictional delineation of real people, particularly those who exerted an almost superhuman control over the fate of their respective generations, includes many factors of which historians cannot claim to be the sole judges. Psychology, a sense of the dramatic, an imagination that can migrate into distant past and bring it to life, and a vital touch of sympathy that can overleap the intervening centuries and find among the people who seem very different from us men and women of flesh and blood like our own. True, Shaw has taken some liberties with history; none-the-less he has given us some fine portraits of historical figures which are real and true to life. His historical plays have given and will give pleasure to countless thousands of readers and theatre-goers.

Notes

1. p. 25.
2. In his letter published in *Public Opinion*, in 1875, Shaw speaks of the 'unreasonable mind of the people'. *The Perfect Wagnerite* reveals the bent of his mind more clearly : 'We have changed our system from Aristocracy to Democracy without considering that we were at the same time changing, as regards our governing class, from Selection to Promiscuity. Those who have taken a practical part in modern politics best know how farcical the result is.' (*Major Critical Essays*, p. 215).
3. Notes to *Caesar and Cleopatra*, p. 201.
4. *The Cult of the Superman*, p. 170.
5. p. x.
6. Preface to *Three Plays for Puritans*, p. xxxi.
7. Eric Bentley, *Bernard Shaw*, p. 78.
8. Allardyce Nicoll, *A History of English Drama*, vol. v, p. 197.
9. Preface to *Saint Joan*, p. 51.
10. Charles Wayland Lightbody, *Judgments of Joan*, p. 33.
11. *What is History*, p. 30.
12. *A Preface to History*, p. 172.
13. *What is History*, p. 13.
14. K.G. Collingwood, *The Idea of History*, p. 56.
15. *History in a Changing World*, p. 14 (Quoted by E.H. Carr in his *What*

    is History, p. 8).

16. *Herr Eugen Dühring's Revolution in Science*, translated by Emil Burns,. p. 31 (Quoted by G.J. Renier in his *History—Its Purpose and Method*,. p. 207).

17. A.C. Danto, *Analytical Philosophy of History*, p. 103.

18. G.J. Renier, *History—Its Purpose and Method*, p. 219.

19. Hesketh Pearson, *G.B.S.: A Postscript*, p. 58.

20. Geoffrey Bullough's letter to me, dated 15 September 1970.

2. The Man of Destiny

I

Shaw's first historical drama, *The Man of Destiny*, is not a great play, but it is a small piece of quality, an entertaining piece. But when it appeared its dramaturgic skill was not noticed by the critics and they condemned it in various terms, and some even thought that to criticise it would be a waste of time and space. The kind of opinion that prevailed against it may be illustrated by the following passage:

> *The Man of Destiny* is less a play than a simple medium for airing of the author's well-known opinions relative to Socialism, political economy, the aggrandisement of England, and other cognate matters. . . . Seriously to criticise a piece of the kind would be consequently a waste of time and space . . . . That there is real cleverness to be found in the dialogue we do not deny, but it is a kind of cleverness, ill-suited to the purposes of the stage.[1]

The passage of time has shown the unjustifiability of such criticisms. *The Man of Destiny* is a fine literary piece and is at the same time instinct with the life of the theatre. In the Preface to *Plays Pleasant* Shaw describes it as 'a bravura piece to display the virtuosity of two principal performers'. The loss of the dispatches, the discovery of the Strange Lady by the Lieutenant, the struggle between Napoleon and the Lady—all these create a dramatic illusion and demand the audience's or the reader's temporary suspension of disbelief. From the very beginning all that happens furthers the action till it comes to an unexpected end. Suspense is maintained throughout and not for one moment is the attention permitted to flag.

The point of the play is the war of wills between Napoleon and the Strange Lady. And the purpose is to show that Napoleon's rise to power was the result not of accident but of certain exceptional mental endowments. Shaw achieves his purpose by using the technique of contrast. The fatuous young aide-de-camp who is duped to believe that the Strange Lady is the sister of the Austrian Officer who robbed him of the dispatches throws into relief Napoleon's clear-sightedness which can see through disguises

The Strange Lady's deference to convention, altruism, and her sex charm are meant to act as a foil to the Man of Destiny's original outlook and his capacity to control the sex-instinct when he has to achieve some goal. And Napoleon's victory is a victory of a will unhampered by any conventions over a will that is bound hand and foot by conventions.

The dialogues are marked by extreme economy and they extend the characterisation and further the action. And some splendid speeches put into the mouth of Napoleon enhance the total effect of the play. Napoleon's speech on fear, on the three sorts of people in the world and on the English character reveal the character of The Man of Destiny and the author's views on certain important things of the world and at the same time the beauty of the ideas they present, their rhetoric and their melody make additional demands on the attention of the audience or the reader.

As Shaw wrote to Ellen Terry, the play displays his 'knowledge of stage tricks'. He was fully conscious of what the public wanted, and he made use of certain elements that make for popularity. 'He was willing and eager to make full and free employment of physical action on the stage—the eternally exciting appeal of melodrama—and to utilise those conceptions which made the burlesque, the farce and the extravaganza once so popular.'[2] This accounts for the coarse and vigorous conversation between Napoleon and Giuseppe with which the play opens, the lieutenant's flamboyant speech beginning with 'Nothing happened to me!', his overexcited speeches and actions to see the Lady, Napoleon's theatrical gesture, pose and action before her. One may feel that Napoleon could get the dispatches without making so much ado, but Shaw knew better, and he exploited the amoristic intrigue and the histrionics of the nineteenth century history play to produce greater theatrical effect and captivate the audience.

II

When Shaw wrote *The Man of Destiny*, Napoleon had become a romantic hero whom sober historians depicted in the grand manner and whom later on Hardy made the protagonist of his enormous epic drama. But *The Man of Destiny* presents this hero in a mere farcical situation. The play, therefore, infuriated many. Mansfield contemptuously declined it and Shaw's French

Translator, Augustin Hamon, said that 'G.B.S. had read all the wrong books about the Emperor'.[3] Sir Henry Irving complained that 'Shaw had no respect for great and distinguished people, and it must have seemed to him that the portrait of Napoleon in *The Man of Destiny* was blasphemous'.[4]

The Man of Destiny is not one of Shaw's great plays, but it is of great interest, because it is his first historical play and because it is in the sketch of Napoleon that the Shavian conception of greatness is revealed, though partially, for the first time. Napoleon, who bestrode Europe like a Colossus for fifteen years, has become a legend, a myth. Popular imagination has transfigured his defects and invested him with attributes almost superhuman. But although innumerable books have been written about his exploits and achievements in the battlefields, few have attempted to depict his inner life, which is the source of his strength and weakness alike, the secret spring of the drama of his marvellous career. Shaw, in *The Man of Destiny*, has caught Napoleon off the battlefield, and through a short and simple incident revealed the strength and weakness of his character. He has taken off all the nimbus, all the illusion that romantic writers have credited him with and like Constant, Premier Valet de Chambre, (in his *Recollections of the Private Life of Napoleon*, an English translation of which appeared in 1895 which Shaw must have read), he has depicted Napoleon *en déshabillé*, as a man, a great man, still a mere man, not a demigod, and no wonder he has been accused of having given a distorted picture of the Emperor.

Napoleon, who has become a legendary figure, has been presented in *The Man of Destiny* as a shabby man of untidy table habits. In the stage direction Shaw describes him thus:

> . . . his elbow has displaced most of the dishes and glasses; and his long hair trails into the risotto when he forgets it and leans more intently over the map.

People whose minds are set on romantic and spectacular plays are naturally offended by such commonplace characteristics in a hero. Shaw has brought the hero off his pedestal, but he has done so in deference to reality. Shaw's description is historically authentic. Napoleon paid no particular attention to his person or dress. After the victory of Lodi 'the people of Milan', says John Holland

Rose, '...gazed with admiration, not unmixed with awe, at the pale features of the young commander, whose plain attire bespoke a Spartan activity ....'[5] Shaw's description corresponds to a drawing of Napoleon by Appiani in 1796, after the battle of Lodi.[6] I am tempted to believe that Shaw had seen and derived his materials from it. Shaw's description is borne out by what Wallace K. Ferguson and Geoffrey Bruun say of him: 'The youthful general of twentyseven who routed the Austrians in Italy was lean, unkempt and shabby, but his sharp gaze could disconcert older and more exprienced officers.'[7] Very few could delve below the surface of Shaw's Napoleon and realise that a very common-place appearance and manner are not incompatible with heroic qualities of character. Indeed, Napoleon's untidy habits throw into brilliant relief the greater traits of his character. His indifference to environment and physical appearance amply testifies to the tremendous power of his mind to concentrate on the immediate object of pursuit. This is undoubtedly a faculty of great minds, and there is ample evidence to show that Napoleon possessed the power of living keenly in the present moment. Roederer, who was his close companion during the Consulate, says, 'That which especially characterises him is the power and persistence of his attention .... I have never seen him distracted from one affair by another, neglecting the matter in hand for one which he is about to work.'[8]

In Shaw's Napoleon there is a union of opposite qualities. He is a realist, but his realism is dashed with streaks of unconscious idealism. Although as a realist he does not respect the rules of war, yet he dignifies 'war with the noise and smoke of cannon, as depicted in all military portraits'. As an original observer he ignores the old fashioned art of war, revolutionising warfare by developing the use of artillery in an unprecedented way. He has 'a clear realistic knowledge of human nature in public affairs'. 'He is imaginative without illusions, and creative without religion, loyalty, patriotism or any of these common ideals.' And yet he is not 'incapable of these ideals: on the contrary, he has swallowed them all in his boyhood, and now, having a keen dramatic faculty, is extremely clever at playing upon them by the arts of the actor and stage manager'. In his portraiture of heroes Shaw has warred on idealism, and the streaks of idealism that we find in his Napoleon are due to his deference to history. For, as J.H. Rose says, 'In the personality of Napoleon nothing is more remarkable than the combination of gifts which in most natures are mutually exclusive.'[9]

Notwithstanding the streaks of idealism, Shaw's view is that it is his realistic and original attitude towards life and the world that constitutes the greatness of Napoleon. As a realist he knows how to exploit a situation, however adverse, to his own advantage. The lack of money, food and clothes for his army would have embarrassed an idealist, but he uses this lack as a means of inciting his soldiers to fight more vigorously so that they may enjoy their natural right to loot the conquered people and thus put an end to their destitution. An original man, Napoleon cannot see eye to eye with others; he disregards routine and defies professional precedents or orders from the Directory. In attributing these qualities to Napoleon in the stage direction Shaw has been faithful to history. J.H. Rose quotes the burning words by which Napoleon incited his soldiers:

> Soldiers, you are half starved and half naked. The Government owes you much, but can do nothing for you. Your patience and courage are honourable to you, but they procure you neither advantage nor glory. I am about to lead you into the most fertile valleys of the world: there you will reap honour, glory and riches. Soldiers of the army of Italy, will you lack courage?[10]

This is how Napoleon incited his army to loot, as Shaw tells us in the stage direction.

Shaw's representation of Napoleon as acting 'on his own responsibility in defiance of professional precedents or orders from Paris' is based on facts. J.H. Rose records that 'Bonaparte's despatches to the Directors were couched in almost imperious terms, which showed that he felt himself the master of the situation.'[11] When the Directory proposed to divide the command in Italy between Napoleon and Killermann, Napoleon replied, '...it was highly impolite to divide the command. Killermann, having more experience would doubtless do it better; but both together would do it very badly.' It was not possible for the Directory to subject the Man of Destiny to the same rules as had been imposed on all French Generals. They drew back, and postponed their decision about dividing the command, and nothing more was heard of this proposal. Napoleon's strategy was unprecedented, and even his own military officers could not seize the subtlety of his warfare. Historians have not succeeded in reducing his strategy to a formula or system. He disregarded routine and tradition, and conducted each campaign with regard to its own requirements. Felix Markham aptly says that 'no two Napoleonic battles are alike'.[12] Shaw does not believe in a specialised military genius. His point is that it was genius diverted into military field that won battles. Julius Caesar and Joan were not professional soldiers and Napoleon won his battles by not following traditional methods. It was their superior insight— the Superman's freedom from illusions that made them great commanders.

Shaw has been accused of having infused into Napoleon something of himself, at least in the stage direction where he says:

> He [Napoleon] has prodigious powers of work and a clear realistic knowledge of human nature in public affairs, having seen it exhaustively tested in that department during the French Revolution....Withal, he is no spoiled child. Poverty, ill luck, the shifts of impecunious shabby-gentility, repeated failure as a would-be author, humiliation as a rebuffed time server; reproof and punishment as an incompetent and dishonest officer, an escape from the service so narrow, that if the emigration of the nobles had not raised the value of even the most rascally lieutenant to the famine price of a general he would have been swept contemptuously from the army; these trials have ground his conceit out of him, and forced him to be self-sufficient and to understand that to such men as he is the world will give nothing that he cannot take from it by force.

This passage gives a picture of Shaw himself, no doubt, but most of the traits of character mentioned here were possessed by Napoleon too. Historians testify to Napoleon's tremendous capacity for work and his superhuman power to endure hardship. Emil Ludwig says, '...he owes his success to youth and health. A body that can endure interminable riding without fatigue, ... a stomach which can digest anything, and makes no complaint at being put on short commons.'[13] Napoleon's early life, like Shaw's was 'associated with nothing but poverty, hardship and defeat'.[14] And like Shaw, Napoleon wrote 'reams of manuscript' and made crude literary efforts. At St. Helena Napoleon said: 'At the age of twenty I sent to the Academy of Lyons various writings which I subsequently withdrew. When I read them I found that their author deserved to be whipped. What ridiculous things I said and how annoyed I would be if they were preserved.'[15] Shaw, it will be evident from our discussion, has been quite faithful to history in the stage directions.

III

Let us now enquire into the play and see how far Shaw's portrait of Napoleon is historically authentic. *The Man of Destiny* deals with a small fictitious incident in the life of Napoleon on 12 May 1796. He is not Emperor yet; he is only a General Commanding the army of Italy. He is putting up in an inn planning his next expedition. Here there is an encounter between him and a Strange Lady—an encounter through which Shaw attempts to reveal the qualities which constitute the greatness of Napoleon and made him Emperor. The exceptional endowments of Napoleon that are revealed here are his realism, his freedom from conventional notions and inhibitions and his masterful will. Shaw implies that it is these superman-like qualities of mind and will that enabled Napoleon to overcome all obstacles both on the field and off the field.

Some despatches which Napoleon has been waiting for have been wheedled out of his lieutenant by a confidence trick played by a lady disguised as an Austrian Officer. Accidentally the lady, no longer disguised, puts up in the inn where Napoleon is staying. The Lieutenant is hoodwinked into the belief that she is the twin sister of the young Austrian Officer. But Napoleon, who is a keen realist, sees through the whole situation in a moment and demands the despatches: 'You tricked that blockhead out of them. You disguised yourself as a man. I want my despatches. They are there in the bosom of your dress, under your hands.'

Now there ensues a struggle for the letters. The lady has come to steal a love letter of Josephine to Director Barras which got mixed up with the official despatches. To achieve her end she proves to be no less formidable a rival to the Man of Destiny than a Wellington or a Pitt. The one is as desperate in her attempts to keep the letters to herself as the other is determined to take them away from her. The struggle between the two is a war of wills. The Lady has outwitted a lieutenant and she would outwit a general. She pretends to weep, she gasps and sighs, she puts on an air of offended delicacy, she tries to win over her opponent by feminine grace and charm, she racks her brains to invent some new device to outwit him. Her wiles would be too strong for an ordinary man to circumvent but they cannot cast any permanent spell on Napoleon, who bullies her and ultimately forces her to yield up all the letters.[16]

Shaw has attributed to Napoleon fixity of purpose and a strong will to realise that purpose. That Napoleon possessed these qualities is conceded by all authorities. 'In the presence of a will so stubborn and genius so fervid', says J.H. Rose, 'what wonder that a friend prophesied that his [Napoleon's] halting place would be either the throne or the scaffold.'[17] Emil Ludwig says, 'Not a sign of arrogance about this conqueror; nothing but resolution and a force of will before which all must bend.'[18]

But it is not so much Napoleon's purpose and will as his original outlook on life and the world that Shaw lays emphasis on. The Lady's purpose and will are as strong as those of Napoleon. Napoleon's superiority, Shaw has shown, lies in his possession of original values, in his immunity from conventional codes of conduct. Indeed, *The Man of Destiny* is a conflict between realism and idealism, between an unconventional outlook and the accepted code of conjugal fidelity. The Lady is chained hand and foot by her morality, respectability and ideals. Moved by humanist feelings, she has come to take away a private letter, which spells dishonour and scandal for an old friend of hers. 'It is only through love, through pity, through the instinct to save and protect someone else, that I can do things that terrify me.' She is good, truthful, unselfish and 'all the rest of it'. She has come to avert an imminent 'domestic scene, a broken household, a public scandal'. Intensely conscious of her respectability, she feels it is not decent on her part to be with Napoleon in that lonely hotel. Napoleon, on the other hand, is never moved by such values; he is essentially mean and selfish, he fights and conquers for himself and for nobody else. He is completely indifferent towards domestic happiness and personal dignity and honour. He has neither conscience nor any scruples. 'Where did you pick up all these vulgar scruples? This (with contemptuous emphasis) conscience of yours?', he asks the Lady. Napoleon is, as the Lady says, 'the vile, vulgar Corsican adventurer'. He is as much above decency as he is above moral scruples, happiness, personal dignity and honour. To get the despatches, he ignores the respect due to the fair sex; he allows no sentimental consideration to stand between him and the letters. When the lady is about to leave the room, he 'rushes at her; seizes her by the arm, and drags her back'. Shaw's Napoleon is a masterful realist, unhampered by any altruism or any conventional code of morality.

The greatest quality of Napoleon in *The Man of Destiny* is that he ultimately proves to be above jealousy. Shaw wrote this immediately after witnessing *Madame Sans-Gene* of M.M. Sardou in Lyceum Theatre on 10 April 1896. He was dissatisfied with Sardou's Napoleon, whom he describes as 'nothing but the Jealous Husband of a thousand fashionable dramas talking Buonapartiana'.[19] Shaw's Napoleon is quite the opposite of the Jealous Husband. The lady, who is conventional to the core, is sure that the revelation in the letter would mean 'a duel with Barras, a domestic scene, a broken household, a public scandal, a checked career, all sorts of things'. Napoleon reads the letter secretly and gives it back to the lady pretending that he has been too magnanimous to read it. He ignores the letter as if it had never existed. He wants to ignore his wife's unchastity and the most dignified way to do it is to pretend he knows nothing about it. It also shows him capable of a meanness which no man guided by conventional morality and etiquette would ever stoop to— stealing into the vineyard and reading the letter. The vulgar Corsican! It may be noted here that Napoleon's attitude to his wife's *liaison* as depicted in this play is in perfect accord with what Constant says in his *Recollections*:

He [Napoleon] said, moreover, that immorality was the most dangerous vice of a sovereign, because of the evil example it set to his subjects. What he meant by *immorality* was doubtless a scandalous publicity given to *liaisons* which might otherwise have remained secret; for as regards these *liaisons* themselves he withstood women no more than any other man when they threw themselves at his head.[20]

The episode of the letter and the encounter between Napoleon and the Strange Lady are invented by Shaw. Josephine was a former mistress of Barras, one of the Directors. Napoleon married her on 9 March 1796, and parted after only two days to command the army of Italy. Shaw imagines that during Napoleon's absence one of the letters of Barras to Josephine got mixed up with the official despatches. He has invented this episode only to reveal the supermanlike qualities that Napoleon possessed and that made him one of the greatest military geniuses of the world.

IV

Shaw's Napoleon possesses most of the ingredients of the Shavian prescription of a great man—realism, originality and will, and their concomitants—fixity of purpose, indifference to personal happiness and dignity, freedom from conscience and moral scruples, disregard for convention, control over self. But, as has already been pointed out, in the opening stage direction he has been presented as a curious amalgam of noble and ignoble impulses. An analysis of the play also reveals that Shaw's Napoleon lacks calmness of character. Napoleon is subject to fury and impatience, and he has not been able entirely to shake off the hypocrisy so characterstic of the middle class. Though he is extremely pleased when the Lady calls him 'a real hero', yet he says, 'Pooh! there is no such thing as a real hero.' He is essentially mean and selfish and in an unguarded moment he admits that he wins battles for himself. But soon he 'pulls himself piously together like a man conducting a religious service' and says, 'I win battles for humanity: for my country, not for myself.' He adds that 'self-sacrifice is the foundation of all true nobility of character'. When the Lady says that she adores him because he is not afraid to be mean and selfish, he indignantly replies that he is neither mean nor selfish. But ultimately he admits that he has no conscience, no scruples, no morality. All this is mere shilly-shallying which a truly great man detests as something beneath him.

Under the insinuation of the lady that the letter in question may compromise his wife with Barras Napoleon loses all control over himself. He is more and more irritated; his face darkens; he walks about in angry perplexity, and furiously whispers, 'This

is your revenge, you she cat, for having had to give me the letters.'
He is exasperated beyond measure; he walks with 'his hands behind
him, his fingers twitching', and he says, 'This woman will drive
me out of my senses.' He calls her 'a detestable woman, and as
ugly as Satan'. He mocks her angrily: 'Ha! ha! ha! What
are you laughing at?' The Lady, who has penetrating insight into
Napoleon's character aptly says, 'I have often seen persons of
your sex getting into a pet and behaving like children; but I never
saw a really great man do it before.' He burns with suspicion;
goes to the vineyard and reads the letter secretly. Although
ultimately he exercises self-control, his behaviour betrays
weaknesses which do not befit a great man. Indeed, here
Napoleon behaves almost as ridiculously as Sergius and James
Mavor Morell behave in similar situations.

Let it be pointed out here that in attributing these weaknesses to
the Man of Destiny Shaw kept close to Napoleon's life. Napoleon
was a man of fiery passion, susceptible to violent jealousy and
petulant outbursts. Constant, who was Napoleon's personal
attendant, has given an authentic description of the precautionary
measures taken by the Emperor to prevent Josephine from meeting
any man except in the presence of witnesses.[21] During the Italian
campaign of 1796 his letters to Josephine also reveal this aspect
of his character. A few extracts will suffice. '...but today the
thought that my Josephine might be ill; and above all, the cruel,
fatal thought that she might love me less blights my soul, stops my
blood, makes me wretched and dejected without ever leaving me the
courage of fury and despair.'[22] 'Have you a lover, have you taken
up with some stripling of nineteen? If so, you have reason to dread
Othello's fist.'[23] 'If I could spend a whole day with you. You
know if I saw a lover with you, I should instantly tear him to
pieces.'[24] But though impetuous and quick tempered, Napoleon
could, and often did, as Shaw's Napoleon does, exercise self-
control by effort. In *The Personality of Napoleon* J.H. Rose
says, 'These two incidents reveal the controlling power of will
over impetuous passion; and herein lay the terror of Napoleon's
wrath, that in the highest transports, it never escaped the grip of
mind and will.'[25] In making Napoleon susceptible to some of the
common weaknesses Shaw has been quite faithful to history where
Napoleon seems to be haunted by jealousy. Shaw's Napoleon,
like the Napoleon of history, is an amalgam of greatness and

weakness, and Shaw's view of greatness is that it co-exists with matter-of-factness, timidity, weaknesses of all sorts—an anti-romantic view of the Hero.

Let us pause here to inquire into Shaw's historical technique. Historical procedure or method consists essentially of interpreting evidence. But *The Man of Destiny* is constructed on an episode for which there is no historical warrant. This episode is especially designed to reveal Napoleon's character, and the salient features of his character have been clearly revealed. The incident is imaginary but the portraiture is correct.

The Man of Destiny is a faithful study of a historical personage by placing him in a situation which is unhistorical. A person who contributed to the making of history cannot be easily isolated from the world he lived in. For a person is the child of his age, acts in conjunction with other people, influences them and is affected by them. The task of all history is to grasp the system of these interactions. For it is the interaction between the depths of human nature and the broad context of historical life that makes true history. But Shaw has not cared to show how Napoleon received stimuli from his environment, was moulded by it and then, in his turn, affected the historical process. In portraying Napoleon he has not taken into account the incidents and circumstances, the facts and forces that make up the stuff of history. Shaw is not a historian but a dramatist, and his emphasis is on character issuing in action, no matter whether the action has a historical basis or not. And he was careful enough to subtitle the play 'A Fictitious Paragraph of History.' This 'fictitious paragraph' was invented to give, and it succeeded in giving, a correct and convincing picture of the Man of Destiny who was soon to become the Emperor of Europe.

Notes

1. *The Theatre*, N.S. XXX, Aug. 1897, 101—2 (Quoted by Allardyce Nicoll in *A History of English Drama*, vol. v, p. 204).
2. Allardyce Nicoll, *A History of English Drama*, vol, v, p. 196.
3. St. John Ervine, *Bernard Shaw: His Life, Work and Friends*, p. 283.
4. Ibid., p. 289.
5. *The Life of Napoleon* (1929), p. 96.

6. Felix Markham, *Napoleon* (1964), illustration no. 3 between pages 146 and 147.
7. *A Survey of European Civilization since* 1500 (1958), p. 624.
8. Quoted by Emil Ludwig in his *Napoleon*, pp. 572–3.
9. *The Life of Napoleon* (1929), p. 77.
10. Ibid., pp. 80–1.
11. Ibid., p. 89.
12. *Napoleon*, p. 26.
13. *Napoleon*, p. 59.
14. Felix Markham, *Napoleon*, p. 1.
15. Ibid., p. 11.
16. The statement of Allardyce Nicoll that 'Napoleon in *The Man of Destiny* is nothing more than a successful captain, easily attracted by a pair of blue eyes' seems to be ill-founded (*British Drama*, p. 438).
17. *The Life of Napoleon*, p. 76.
18. *Napoleon*, p. 68.
19. *Our Theatres in the Nineties*, vol. III, p. 110.
20. Vol. I, p. 409.
21. *Recollections*, vol. II, pp. 271–3.
22. J.H. Rose, *The Personality of Napoleon* (1919), p. 21.
23. Emil Ludwig, *Napoleon*, p. 71.
24. Ibid., p. 72.
25. p. 32.

3. Caesar and Cleopatra

I

Shaw's second historical play, *Caesar and Cleopatra*, is a much weightier and more impressive work than his first venture, *The Man of Destiny*. The purpose of the play is to draw a great man in history. '*Caesar and Cleopatra* is the first and only adequate dramatisation of the greatest man that ever lived. I want to revive, in a modern way and with modern refinement, the sort of thing that Booth did the last of in America: the projection on the stage of the hero in the big sense of the word.'[1] Shaw was highly dissatisfied with Shakespeare's sketch of Julius Caesar in the tragedy bearing his name. Shakespeare's Caesar is a relatively minor character speaking no more than 120 lines, and he is dispatched by assassins soon after the play begins. It seems to have been Shakespeare's desire to portray Caesarism rather than Caesar. His presentation of Caesar as an irritable, pompous, deaf old man was a blasphemy in the opinion of Shaw, who had a great admiration for Caesar. In the Preface he says, 'Shakespeare, who knew human weakness so well, never knew human strength of the Caesarian type. His Caesar is an admitted failure.' And he offered his Caesar as an improvement on Shakespeare's.

Shaw has taken up Caesar's Egyptian war, the most difficult and dangerous war Caesar had ever undertaken, for the theme of his drama. As Roman consul Caesar arrives in Egypt to settle a dynastic dispute between young Ptolemy and his sister-wife Cleopatra and to exact the tribute the father of the two rivals owed to Rome. Soon he finds himself entangled in a dangerous conflict with the Egyptian soldiers, the city mob and the Roman army of occupation under the leadership of Achillas. He is in a foreign country vastly outnumbered by a well equipped and cunning enemy, the north west wind prevailing at this season of the year is unfavourable to him; all his communications by sea have been cut off and he has been deprived of all drinking water; in a short time he and his troops are faced with the danger of imminent destruction. But though caught off his guard and though without sufficient troops, Caesar by his customary resourcefulness, brilliant improvisation and personal bravery, makes head against a great city and a powerful army, and wins victory. Ultimately he collects 16,000 talents, establishes Cleopatra queen to rule over Egypt under Roman supremacy, appoints Rufio as the Roman Governor and returns to Rome.

Caesar and Cleopatra has many commendable qualities, and in some respects it is one of the most remarkable modern historical plays. Though it flouts the conventional romantic history play by keeping love off the stage, it exploits elaborate spectacle and flamboyant histrionics of the nineteenth century history play. On 15 December 1898 when he had just finished the play, Shaw wrote to Golding Bright that the play 'is in five acts, containing eight scenes, and involving considerable variety and splendour of mounting'.[2] Martin Meisel aptly says about this play: 'Costume and crowds, scenery and spectacle, were thoroughly in the line of the nineteenth century treatment of history on the stage not only as an elementary part of audience appeal but as the adjuncts of a heroic atmosphere.'[3]

Shaw's skill in drawing characters is revealed in this play, especially in drawing the character of the protagonist—Caesar round whom the action of the play centres. The greatness of Caesar is revealed through a number of contrasts. In the first three acts Caesar is Cleopatra's teacher, teaching her how a queen should behave. In the last two acts she is found to have gained in dignity and wisdom through contact with the greatness of Caesar. But as she has developed revengeful passion and erotic passion, she becomes Caesar's antagonist and stands as a contrast to the protagonist, who has no such passions. The men about Caesar—Rufio, Achillas, Pothinus and others—with their conventional attitude and irritable temper throw into bold relief Caesar's originality and composure. The contrast between Caesar and Theodotus in their attitude towards the burning of the library of Alexandria is a contrast between a maker of history and a historian, between a creator of environment and a creature of environment, between a man of decision and a man who has no decision.

Caesar is an exceptional human being in whom we find a harmonious blending of many contrary elements. He is a conqueror whose business it is to conquer countries by cruel bloodshed, but he is full of clemency and is averse to murder. He is passionate and is dazzled by the eyes of women but his passion is completely under his control and no woman has any control over him. He is a practical man of the world adroitly busy in conquering countries and settling disputes, but his deeper self finds real pleasure in dreaming and he 'will conquer ten continents to pay for dreaming it out to the end'. And though he is a dreamer he tells the Egyptians not to dream their lives away with the help of books, for, although he is an author himself he does not hesitate to burn the library of Alexandria which is the past memory of mankind, and he will destroy the past only to build the future with its ruins.

Cleopatra, the charming minx, who even at the age of sixteen 'troubles men's minds' and likes 'men, especially young men with round strong arms', who in the space of six months rapidly matures and plots to rule her conqueror and admits that she loves not a god like Caesar but a man like Antony— 'one who can love and hate—one whom I can hurt and who would hurt me', is a flesh and blood reality. Caesar's secretary Britannus and Cleopatra's head nurse Ftatateeta are two more memorable characters in the play, and 'since they owe nothing to historical models they are more significant dramatic creations'.

There is a number of poetical passages in *Caesar and Cleopatra*— Caesar's apostrophe to the Sphinx which is followed by his anti-climactic reception by Cleopatra, his speech on vengeance beginning with 'Vengeance! Vengeance! Oh, if I could stoop to vengeance', his outburst at the wanton murder of Pothinus which makes him visualise with horror a future in which 'murder shall breed murder, always in the name of right and honour and peace, until the gods are tired of blood and create a race that can understand'. The Prologue spoken by an 'august personage' from within the dark temple of Ra is marked by 'poetic dignity of movement, reminiscent of the rising and falling cadences of the Old Testament prophetic books in the English Authorized Version, and therefore harking back, however remotely, to Hebrew poetry'.[4] There is a conflict between the comic spirit that springs from the intellect and poetry which springs from heart, but in Shaw's works we often find a happy blending of the two. Then Caesar's utterances such as 'Pompey's head has fallen; and Caesar's is ripe', 'I have always disliked the idea of dying: I had rather be killed', 'and I will send you a man, Roman from head to heel and Roman of the noblest; not old and ripe for the knife', spell his assassination and make a touching appeal.

II

Caesar and Cleopatra is an attempt at the portraiture of a truly great man. It is Shaw's ninth play, but it is here, in the character of Caesar, that we get for the first time a clear idea of his conception of a great man. Caesar is Shaw's greatest character thus far. He is a man of rare magnanimity and power; he is a master not only of his mind but also of his environments; he has a purpose of his own and he is endowed with a tremendous will which enables him to manipulate things and beings for the accomplishment of his purpose; he is possessed of wonderful restraint and clemency; he is immune from the weaknesses which common flesh is heir to; he is, says Shaw, naturally great. 'Shakespeare's Caesar might have been a successful importer of bananas: Shaw's is a genius whose every speech has the sound of a genius.'[5] Shaw's Ceasar is a very great man but is he the real Julius Caesar? Shaw says, 'Shakespeare's Caesar is the *reductio ad absurdum* of the real Julius Caesar. My Caesar is a simple return to nature and history.'[6] But, as will be pointed out in the following pages, Shaw's Caesar is in many respects a different man from the Caesar of history.

Shaw has represented Caesar as too great to find any joy and peace in this world. Though as a general he has to remain constantly busy with wars and conquests, his real self is far from being satisfied with such activities. He belongs to a different world, as it were, and walks 'the earth with a sort of stern levity, lightly touching the planet and yet spurning it away like a stone. He walks like a winged man who has chosen to fold his wings.'[7] He is intensely conscious of the futility and vulgarity of his occupation as a soldier, and occasionally turns away from reality to live in contemplation of the constant and immortal part of his life. He is a being apart, and conscious of his great superiority to humanity, he feels lonely, as lonely as the Sphinx in the vast Egyptian desert, whom he addresses thus:

Hail, Sphinx: Salutation from Julius Caesar! I have wandered in many lands, seeking the lost regions from which my birth into this world exiled me, and the company of creatures such as myself. I have found flocks and pastures, men and cities, but no other Caesar, no air native to me, no man kindred to me, none who can do my day's deed, and think my night's thought. In the little world yonder, Sphinx, my place is as high as yours in the great desert....Sphinx, you and I, strangers to the race of men, are no strangers to one another....

The Sphinx is the symbol of Caesar's genius: 'part brute, part woman, and part God—nothing of man in me at all'.

Shaw's Caesar is one of the greatest experiments of the Life Force; as Dr. Sengupta says, 'the evolutionary instinct is never dormant in him'.[8] He feels that his great soul is being cramped within the narrow confines of his profession. He is sick of Rome. He says, 'What has Rome to show me that I have not seen already? One year of Rome is like another, except that I grow older, whilst the crowd in the Appian Way is always the same age.' He is sick of a warrior's profession. He tells Rufio, 'Oh, this military life! this tedious, brutal life of action! That is the worst of us Romans: we are mere doers and drudgers: a swarm of bees turned into men.' Apollodorus aptly describes him as not 'merely the conquering soldier but the creative poet artist'. A great creative genius, Caesar loathes war which is a force of destruction. He is a dreamer and what would he not pay for a beautiful dream? Standing before the Sphinx in the vast moonlit desert, he hears a girl's voice and thinks that he is dreaming and he says to himself: 'What a dream! What a magnificent dream! Only let me not wake, and I will conquer ten continents to pay for dreaming it out to the end.' He is sick of Rome, he is sick of the world. He is a visionary, longing to build a new kingdom, a holy city free from the vulgar pursuits of this world. He cries out, 'Cleopatra: will you come with me and track the flood to its cradle in the heart of the regions of mystery? Shall we leave Rome behind us—Rome, that had achieved greatness only to learn how greatness destroys nations of men who are not great! Shall I make you a new kingdom, and build you a holy city there in the great unknown?' These are the utterances of a poet and mystic, living an active life but with one part of his soul always looking upward to the ideal world of his dream. Shaw has given us a few fleeting glimpses of this mystic, poetic Caesar, who is so different not only from his fellows but also from himself as he appears to the world.

Shaw, it will be evident from our discussion, has attributed to Caesar the qualities of absolute disinterestedness in worldly affairs, freedom from worldly ambition and aversion to political and military glory. Also in his notes following the play he says, 'Indeed it is clear from his [Caesar's] whole history that what has been called his ambition was an instinct for exploration. He had much more of Columbus and Franklin in him than of Henry V.' But the Caesar of history did not possess the qualities Shaw has credited him with. History provides ample evidence that Julius Caesar had a burning ambition for political and military eminence and glory. Coming upon a statue of Alexander the Great in Spain, he reproached himself for having accomplished so little at an age when the Macedonian had conquered half the Mediterranean world. While in Spain he devoted his leisure hours to reading the history of Alexander; this made him very pensive and at last he burst into tears. As his friends were wondering what might be the reason, he said, 'Do you think I have no sufficient cause for concern when Alexander at my age reigned over so many conquered countries, and I have not one glorious achievement to boast?'[9] Caesar had an unquenchable thirst for power, conquest and glory. Plutarch speaks, in his wonderful style, of Caesar's ever increasing passion for fresh renown: 'Caesar had such talents for great attempts, and so vast an ambition, that the many actions he had performed by no means induced him to sit down and enjoy the glory he had acquired: they rather whetted his appetite for other conquests....and inspired him with a passion for fresh renown, as if he had exhausted all the pleasures of the old. This passion was nothing but a jealousy of himself, a contest with himself (as eager as if it had been with another man) to make the future achievements outshine the past.'[10] Not only had Caesar an unquenchable ambition, but to fulfil his ambition he wove a network of political intrigues and conspiracies. In 65 B.C. Caesar plotted with Marcus Crassus, Publius Sulla and Lucius Antonius to attack the Senate House, kill as many senators as convenient, and usurp political power. He had complicity in the conspiracy of 63 B.C. associated with the name of Catiline. When he had no resource left, he secured popular support by enormous bribes. For example, to get the office of the Chief Pontiff, he 'used most flagrant bribery'.[11] His limitless desire for his own advancement to power and for the achievement of personal glory has been beautifully brought out by Suetonius: 'Not only did he [Caesar] accept unconstitutional honours, such as life consulship, a life dictatorship, a perpetual censorship, the title "Emperor"

put before his name, and the title "Father of his Country" appended
to it, also a statue standing among those of the ancient Kings, and
a raised couch placed in the orchestra at the Theatre; but took other
honours which, a mere mortal, he should certainly have refused.
These included a golden throne in the Senate House, and another
on the Tribunal; a ceremonial Chariot and litter for carrying his
statue in the religious procession around the Circus; temples,
altars and divine images; a priest of his own cult; a new college of
Lupercals to celebrate his divinity; and the renaming of the seventh
month as "July". Few, in fact, were the honours which he was not
pleased to accept or assume.'[12] Caesar stamped his own image
upon Roman coins— 'an unprecedented insolence', and wore a
King's robes of purple. 'At the Lupercalia, on 15 February 44,
the consul Antony, sacerdotally naked and impiously drunk tried
thrice to place a royal crown upon Caesar's head. Thrice Caesar
refused; but was it not because the crowd murmured disapproval?
Did he not dismiss from office the Tribunes who removed from his
statue the royal diadem placed upon it by his friends?... many
patricians feared that any day might see him proclaimed a king.'[13]
These things are not the symptoms of a mind that is free from
ambitions and averse to worldly glory. On the contrary, these
are the symptoms of the megalomania of a man who has applied
himself heart and soul to achieve, by hook or by crook, political
and military eminence. Mommsen, who is Shaw's source, has
diluted Caesar's rationalism with occasional mysticism and his
worldliness with a tinge of unworldliness. Shaw has taken a hint
from him and transformed the ambitious adventurer, Caesar,
into an unworldly mystic, an exile into this world which he spurns.

III

Shaw's Caesar has some marked similarities with his creator.
There is always something about Shaw which suggests that in a
better civilisation 'he would have been a great saint. He would
have been a saint of a sternly ascetic, perhaps of a sternly negative
type. But he has this strange note of the saint in him; that he is
literally unworldly. Worldliness has no human magic for him;
he is not bewitched by rank nor drawn on by conviviality at all.'[14]
Shaw has drawn a portrait of himself in Caesar by representing him
as an unworldly man, a dreamer dreaming of perfection not to be

found here. But in this silly, chaotic world, Shaw was a man of business sagacity, sufficient to himself and strong enough to dispense with happiness. This trait of Shaw's character is also seen in Caesar. Caesar, whose deeper self loves to turn away from this world, is found to be adroitly busy with the affairs of the world. These two contradictory elements have been blended together in the character of the conqueror.

Shaw's Caesar, like Mommsen's, is 'a thorough realist'. Indeed, the secret of his greatness is his realistic attitude to life and the world. To this realism he owes his magnanimity and clemency, his lack of resentment at treachery, his freedom from malice against a vanquished enemy, his indifference to idealism and, above all, his success in diplomacy and war. It is due to this realism that Caesar always stands aloof from all ideology and everything fanciful, and it is this realism that never allows age old traditions to disturb him. His complete disregard of routine and tradition often brings him into conflict with the men around him. But as is the case with a realist, he always has his way.

In his sketch of Julius Caesar, Shaw has laid great emphasis on the conqueror's magnanimity and clemency. If in a nature so harmoniously organised any one aspect may be singled out as characteristic, it is that he has a great soul. Though a conqueror by profession, human sympathy always occupies a large part of his heart. Bel Affris, a young nobleman of the court of Cleopatra, who brings tidings of the near approach of Caesar and the Romans, narrates that Caesar after defeating the Egyptians, treated them with respect. Caesar treats little Ptolemy and Cleopatra with fatherly affection. He is not disturbed by the impertinent remarks of Pothinus, Theodotus and Achillas:

POTHINUS. . . Caesar has been defeated before and may be defeated again. A few weeks ago Caesar was flying for his life before Pompey: a few months hence he may be flying for his life before Cato and Juba of Numidia, the African King.

ACHILLAS. (*following up Pothinus's speech menacingly*) What can you do with 4,000 men?

THEODOTUS. (*following up Achillas's speech with a raucous squeak*) And without money? Away with you.

ALL THE COURTIERS. (*shouting fiercely and crowding towards Caesar*) Away with you, Egypt for the Egyptians! Begone.

Rufio bites his beard, too angry to speak. Caesar sits as comfortably as if he were at breakfast, and the cat were clamoring jor a piece of Finnan-haddie.

CLEOPATRA. Why do you let them talk to you like that, Caesar? Are you afraid?

CAESAR. Why, my dear, what they say is quite true.

Not only does Caesar remain undisturbed by such arrogance of the Egyptians but shows boundless clemency to them. Britannus announces that all the Egyptians in the palace are Caesar's prisoners, but Caesar declares that they are his guests, and that they are free to go, and Rufio is indignant that Caesar in his clemency, forbears to capture the Egyptians. Caesar describes as natural not only an insinuation of Pothinus but also Cleopatra's treachery against him. He magnanimously refuses to read the letters revealing the names of the enemies who plotted against him since he crossed the Rubicon. Caesar's clemency and magnanimity are best revealed in his attitude to vengeance. Every word of his condemnation of the murder of Pompey has the ring of sincerity: 'Vengeance! Vengeance! Oh, if I could stoop to vengeance, what would I not exact from you as the price of this murdered man's blood? (They shrink back, appalled and disconcerted). Was he not my son-in-law, my ancient friend, for 20 years the master of great Rome, for 30 years the compeller of victory? Did not I, as a Roman, share his glory? Was the Fate that forced us to fight for the mastery of the world, of our making? Am I Julius Caesar, or am I a wolf, that you fling to me the gray head of the old soldier, the laurelled conqueror, the mighty Roman, treacherously struck down by this callous ruffian, and then claim my gratitudes for it (to Lucius Septimus) Begone: you fill me with horror.' His denunciation of vengeance when he learns that Cleopatra has had Pothinus murdered is superb: 'You have slain their leader : it is right that they shall slay you. If you doubt it, ask your four counsellors here. And then in the name of that right (he emphasizes the word with great scorn) shall I not slay them for murdering their queen, and be slain in my turn by their countrymen as the invader of their fatherland? Can Rome do less than slay these slayers, too, to shew the world how Rome avenges her sons and her honor. And so, to the end of history, murder shall breed murder, always in the name of right and honor and peace, until the gods are tired of blood and create a race that can understand.' Towards the close of the play Cleopatra penetratingly describes Caesar's way of ruling as 'without punishment. Without revenge. Without judgment.'

Magnanimity and clemency, two very outstanding qualities of the character of Shaw's Caesar, should be seen in their proper perspective. A careful examination reveals that these qualities are only offshoots of his realism, his freedom from ideals, his anti-romantic attitude to life. A realist in the deepest sense of the term, Caesar sees further than other men and sees things as they are. His judgment is never clouded by romantic and sentimental considerations. And he has no illusion about his own powers and limitations. The Roman general ruling in the Alexandrian palace, his peremptory requisition of old debts and his intervention in the dispute for the throne are all highly exasperating to the Egyptians. The north west wind is opposed to his return to Rome, the reinforcement, ordered by him from Asia, will take a long time to arrive, King Ptolemy's army outnumbers his own little troop a hundred to one, and in numerous cases his soldiers have been mercilessly assassinated in the city by the exasperated multitude. Caesar is realist enough to sense the immense danger in which he is placed with his small force and no money. He even repents that he has come to Egypt: 'The Egyptians cannot be such fools as not to storm the barricade and swoop down on us here before it is finished. It is the first time I have ever run an avoidable risk. I should not have come to Egypt.' In such circumstances, the realist Caesar must show magnanimity and clemency to the enemy, for malevolence and vengefulness would, by infuriating a far superior power, bring his own destruction and the destruction of his men. He pats Ptolemy with fatherly affection, deals with the Egyptians with the utmost indulgence, and thus succeeds in enjoining the belligerent brother and sister to suspend hostilities. He releases Ptolemy in the hope that his clemency towards the king may allay the insurrection outside. He lets Theodotus go to save the library, because 'every Egyptian we imprison means imprisoning two Roman soldiers to guard him'. And Rufio says, 'Agh! I might have known there was some fox's trick behind your fine talking.' He sets Pothinus free, because there are enough mouths to be fed without him. He magnanimously refuses to read the letters which passed between Pompey's party and the army of occupation in Alexandria, because he cannot afford to waste the next three years of his life in proscribing and condemning men who will now be his friends.

That Caesar's magnanimity and clemency are offshoots of his realistic attitude to life is best illustrated in his attitude towards vengeance. He violently denounces the murder of Pompey, because by his death he loses more than he gains. Pompey was a very popular ruler of Rome for twenty years, and so his hold over the people cannot perish with his death. Under the leadership of his two sons, Gnaeus and Sextus, the Pompeians are sure to avenge their leader's murder. Caesar is realist enough to apprehend it. His outburst against Pompey's murder is genuine, and Dr. Sengupta's statement that Caesar 'has not disrelished it',[15] cannot bear examination. Caesar's attitude to Pompey's murder is based on Mommsen who says, 'He [Caesar] turned away in deep agitation when the murderer brought the head of his rival to his ship. How Caesar would have dealt with Pompeius had he been captured alive it is impossible to say. But interest as well as humanity would probably have counselled clemency.'[16]

Caesar sets Pothinus free only to be saved from the 'Egyptian Red Sea of Blood'. He is furious at the murder of Pothinus, because as a realist he knows that the murder of this favourite of the people is sure to be avenged by the whole city. He delivers a fine speech denouncing vengeance but shortly we find him justifying the murder of Ftatateeta by saying that it was a 'natural slaying' done without judgement. Has not Rufio *judged* it necessary to do away with the blood-drunk nurse of Cleopatra? There is absolutely no difference between the motive of Rufio and the motive of Cleopatra. Each is actuated by a desire to get rid of a potential nuisance. Caesar's justification of the murder of Ftatateeta is only an attempt to make the worse appear the better reason. Almost in the same breath he denounces the murder of Pothinus and defends the murder of Ftatateeta, because, as Dr. Sengupta beautifully puts it, 'the murder of Pothinus rouses the Egyptians to vengeance, but Ftatateeta's death can do nothing more than make the helpless queen wear mourning'.[17] All that clearly emerges is that Caesar's clemency and magnanimity are offshoots of his realism. Here Shaw has taken a hint from Mommsen: 'His clemency and his indifference were not the fruit of sentiment, but of the statesmanly conviction that vanquished parties are absorbed within the state more rapidly than they can be exterminated by proscription.'[18]

We may pause here for a moment to examine how far Shaw is historically justified in attributing magnanimity and clemency to Caesar. Nobody can deny that all his life Caesar behaved with wonderful restraint and clemency. He was singularly tolerant of all opposition, and nearly always pardoned his enemies. 'Whereas Pompey declared that all who were not actively with him were against him and would be treated as public enemies, Caesar announced that all who were not actively against him were with him. He allowed every centurion whom he had appointed on Pompey's recommendation to join the Pompeian forces if he pleased.'[19] The Pompeian general Afranius massacred every Caesarian soldier found in his camp. Yet after capturing him Caesar let him go free. He bade his men spare all Romans who should surrender and as to Brutus, he ordered they were to capture him without injuring him, or else they were to let him escape. He also forgave Cassius at the request of Brutus. To the nations of the East, who had supported Pompey, he was likewise lenient. He not only pardoned most of those who had appeared against him in the field, but on some of them he bestowed honours and preferments. The statues of Pompey were thrown down by the crowds of Rome but Caesar erected them again. After the Egyptian war the enemies sued for peace, and their submission was met with clemency. Even Pompey paid a glorious tribute to Caesar when he advised the citizens of Mytilene to submit to the conqueror, for he said, 'Caesar was a man of great goodness and clemency.' Being defeated at Thaprus Cato committed suicide after advising his son to submit to Caesar. And Caesar 'mourned that he had no chance to pardon Cato, he could only pardon his son'.

No doubt Caesar was not naturally vindictive. But his hatred of vengeance has been exaggerated by Shaw. There is evidence to show that on several occasions he showed a great desire for vengeance. On his way to Rhodes he was caught by pirates. He behaved with them with consummate nonchalance, and when released, he lost no time in cutting their throats. 'Caesar loved his men dearly; when news came that Titurius's command had been massacred, he swore neither to cut his hair nor to trim his beard until they had been avenged.'[20] Shaw in his play has represented

Caesar as violently denouncing the murder of Pothinus, but it was really Caesar who got him murdered: 'Learning from his barber that Pothinus and the Egyptian general Achillas were plotting to kill him and slaughter the small force that he had brought with him, he delicately arranged the assassination of Pothinus. Achillas escaped to the Egyptian army and roused it to insurrection; soon all Alexandria was alive with soldiers vowing death to Caesar.'[21] Shaw is a proponent of the Superman theory. A Shavian Superman possesses freedom of will not only in controlling the outward events of his life but also in controlling the inward temper in which he faces these events. By attributing to Caesar the power to preserve inward integrity and balance of mind in circumstances which call forth the spirit of vengeance and upset ordinary human beings, Shaw has ignored historical evidence, and he has done so to make Caesar conform to a Superman of his conception.

Caesar's men cannot see eye to eye with him. What is considered as expedient by him is always looked down upon by others as inexpedient and even suicidal. This is because Caesar is a realist. He does not see as other men see; he sees better. It is this realism that accounts for his complete disregard of routine and tradition, and enables him to find the proper means for every end with the certainty of divination. Thus during the Alexandrian war he ignores military tradition and burns the fleet which cannot be placed in safety. Rufio is amazed but the realist must burn the ships if by doing so a position of defence can be secured. It is the end rather than the means that he is concerned with. He is determined to win the war, and every other consideration must give way to what is necessary for the attainment of this end. The library of Alexandria, the first of the seven wonders of the world, must burn because the fire, by distracting the enemy, helps him to capture the island of Pharos. In the ultimate analysis, it is this realistic attitude that is found to be the secret of his success in the Egyptian war, and Rufio ultimately admits that the realist's way 'is the right way, the great way, the only possible way in the end'.

Caesar's capture, loss and recapture of the island of Pharos, his swimming for his life, the story of Apollodorus carrying Cleopatra in a carpet to Caesar, the burning of the fleet, the fire of which consumed a great portion of the Alexandrian library are all historical incidents. But the centre of Shaw's interest is not the

historical narrative but the character of the protagonist. He is
a dramatist who meets the exigencies of the theatre and throws into
bold relief the character of the protagonist even by making changes
in the historical incidents. With him incidents have no importance
of their own but are subordinated to the portraiture of character
and the organisation of the play.

IV

Caesar and Cleopatra is one of the three plays for Puritans. It
is a play for Puritans in that it is anti-romantic. The play is a
counterblast to Shakespeare's *Antony and Cleopatra* in which
unmitigated lust has been poetised into heroism. Shakespeare has
made a hero of a hog like Antony who runs away from the
battlefield for love of Cleopatra and loses an empire for slavery to
lust. This was intolerable, blasphemous to Shaw. And he wrote
Caesar and Cleopatra to set off a man of infinite capacity for work,
a man of tremendous self-control, Caesar, against Antony, whose
unbridled sexual infatuation brought about his ruin. Shaw has
kept Eros at an arm's length. 'Whoever, then, expects to find
Cleopatra a Circe and Caesar a hog in these pages, had better lay
down my book and be spared the disappointment.'[22]
    Shaw's Caesar is a man of passion, but his passion is never
stronger than he can control. That his nature is passionate
is amply testified to by the speeches of others as well as by some of
his own speeches. His extreme sensitiveness to the call of sex is
known even to foreign countries. The Persian guardsman says
that Caesar is a great lover of women; Ptolemy and Pothinus fear
that it will not be difficult for Cleopatra to cast a spell on Julius
Caesar and get back her country from him 'with her kisses'. He
often stoops to the meanest subterfuge to win the heart of a pretty
girl; Rufio, Caesar's shield, who knows him so intimately, says that
he always celebrates his birthday when there is a pretty girl to be
flattered. In the first meeting before the Sphinx, when Cleopatra
does not know that she is talking with Caesar, Caesar tells her
that he 'is easily deceived by women. Their eyes dazzle him; and
he sees them not as they are, but as he wishes them to appear to him.'
He is intensely conscious of his age, of the wrinkles on his visage
and of his bald head, and at the same time he exclaims: 'And my
child's heart!' But Caesar, a man of passion, is not a slave of

passion. The beautiful and clever minx, Cleopatra, spares no
effort to captivate her judge, but Caesar only amuses himself by
petting and fondling her. He is in a grave situation and he would
not allow himself to be beglamoured by a woman. He tells
Cleopatra that her life matters little to him and that when the
trumpet sounds, he will hold the hand of the meanest soldier more
sacred than her head. She tells Pothinus: '...Caesar loves no
one. He has no hatred in him: he makes friends with everyone
as he does with dogs and children. His kindness is a wonder.'
When Pothinus asks whether Cleopatra loves him, she replies,
'Can one love a God?'

Shaw has, thus, presented Caesar as a man with a tremendous
control over his passion, allowing no woman, not even Cleopatra,
to exercise any influence over him when there was a grave task
ahead of him. He has also shown that the love between Caesar
and Cleopatra was a trifling affair. In all this Shaw has taken
hints from Mommsen for his facts, flouting all classical authorities.
Mommsen says:

> He [Caesar] had had his season of youth, and song, love and wine
> had taken lively possession of his spirit; but with him they did
> not penetrate to the inmost core of his nature....Around him,
> as around all those whom the full lustre of woman's love has
> dazzled in youth, fainter glimpse of it continued imperishably
> to linger; even in later years he had love-adventures and
> successes with women, ... But, however much even when
> monarch he enjoyed the society of women, he only amused
> himself with them, and allowed them no manner of influence
> over him; even his much censured relation with Cleopatra was
> only contrived to mask a weak point in his political position.[23]

It may be pointed out here that Mommsen makes Caesar's passion
for Cleopatra a policy of expediency while Shaw represents this
passion as a dream, not an infatuation, which has nothing to do
with expediency.

As regards his power to control the instinct of sex and his love
episode with Cleopatra, Shaw's picture of Caesar, which is
essentially based on Mommsen, is entirely different from the real
Caesar. The virtue of complete mastery over sexual passion which
Shaw has attributed to Caesar is a myth. Ample evidence is

provided by classical authorities that Julius Caesar was a man of
hot sexual impulses—a dissolute man, gratifying his sex instinct
by extravagant and indiscriminate indulgences. Suetonius has
given a long list of Roman Matrons—wives of Roman
nobles whom he had seduced.[24] Among his mistresses, says
Suetonius, there were also several queens, the most famous among
whom was Cleopatra. Scandals about his indiscriminate illicit
relation with women clustered thick about him, and many ribald
verses were composed and sung throughout Rome. During his
Gallic Triumph the following song was popular:

Home we bring our bald whoremonger;
Romans, lock your wives away!
All the bags of gold you lent him
Went his Gallic tarts to pay.[25]

He carried on many sexual affairs at the same time, and changed
his mistresses as his fancy dictated. It was rumoured that Brutus
was really Caesar's son. Plutarch says that Caesar believed
Brutus to be his son. 'Possibly Brutus himself shared this opinion,
and hated the dictator for having seduced his mother and made
him, in the gossip of Rome, a bastard instead of the Brutus.'[26]
Whatever the truth about this scandal, Servilia, Brutus' mother
was the woman he loved best and she held him longer than any
other woman, and it was gossiped that in later years she was induced
to surrender her daughter Tertia to Caesar's lust. Servilia, a
woman of insatiable sexual passion, 'sapped his strength until he
was in danger of physical collapse'.[27] The real Caesar, it will be
evident, is not at all like the Man of Destiny whom Shaw has
credited with tremendous power to control the instinct of sex.
    Shaw has attached no seriousness to the love between Caesar
and Cleopatra. In the Preface he makes Ra say:

Are ye impatient with me? Do ye crave for a story of an
unchaste woman? Hath the name of Cleopatra tempted ye
hither? Ye foolish ones; Cleopatra is yet but a child that is
whipped by her nurse. And what I am about to show you for
the good of your souls is how Caesar, seeking Pompey in Egypt,
found Cleopatra...and what things happened between the
old Caesar and the child queen before he left Egypt....

Shaw's Cleopatra is sixteen when Caesar meets her for the first time. But though she is not yet a woman, she, as the Persian guardsman says, 'already troubles men's wisdom'. Caesar, on the other hand, looks upon her as a child; he always addresses her as a 'little kitten', 'my poor child', and pets and fondles her only to amuse himself. She plays so insignificant a part in his life that he forgets her completely on the eve of his departure for Rome. Caesar asks Rufio, 'And now, what else have I to do before I embark? (*Trying to recollect*) There is something I cannot remember : What can it be? Well, well: it must remain undone: we must not waste this favourable wind.' However, as Caesar makes his farewells and proceeds towards the gangway, Cleopatra comes there, 'cold and tragic, cunningly dressed in black', and says, 'Has Cleopatra no part in this leave-taking?' Caesar, who had forgotten all about her, says, 'Ah, I knew there was something. (To Rufio) How could you let me forget her, Rufio? (Hastening to her) Had I gone without seeing you, I should never have forgiven myself.'.

Shaw has given a completely new picture of the love between Caesar and Cleopatra. He has made Cleopatra sixteen though, in fact, she was twenty-one at the time of Caesar's arrival in Egypt. According to Mommsen, whom Shaw has followed, she was nineteen when Caesar met her for the first time. Shaw must have deliberately made Cleopatra younger by five years only to suggest that the existence of any serious love between a girl of sixteen and an old man of fifty is absurd. Following Mommsen faithfully, he says, through the mouth of Ra, that 'Caesar, seeking Pompey in Egypt, found Cleopatra'. This is far from the truth. From Rome Caesar had heard stories about the beauty and disdainful pride of Cleopatra. He had a great liking for exotic queens, and stories about the Egyptian queen must have aroused in him a strong temptation to seek her out and conquer her heart. Cleopatra, as Ludwig says, 'felt sure that it was she, and not the hunted Pompey, whom Caesar had come to seek on the shores of Egypt'.[28] The tax he wanted to collect lay in the treasury in Alexandria where he was and not in Syria where Cleopatra was obliged to take her abode, and yet he sent for her, not once but twice! And from the day she was smuggled into the palace in a carpet by Apollodorus, her conquest of Caesar, as Plutarch says,[29] advanced fast.

The old passionate conqueror had too inextricably entangled

himself with the young and subtle queen. During his absence
everything in Rome was in a state of dissolution. He was badly
wanted there, and as soon as the Egyptian war was over, messenger
after messenger was sent calling him back to Rome. But Caesar
continued in Egypt for nine months fascinated by Cleopatra. At
the end of Shaw's play Caesar promises to send her Mark Antony
saying, 'I will not forget. Farewell: I do not think we shall meet
again. Farewell.' The fact is that Cleopatra followed Caesar
to Rome, where she bore him a son. Caesar even allowed her to
call the son Caesarion. He set up the statue of Cleopatra as
Venus. He also issued a coin on which Venus and Eros could be
recognised as Cleopatra with Caesar in her arms. And 'the
scandal ran that Caesar meant to marry her, a foreigner and a queen
and to rule as King at Alexandria'.[30] But in Shaw's play the love
between Caesar and Cleopatra is a trifling affair, so trifling indeed
that in the rush of preparation on the eve of his departure for
Rome, Caesar forgets her very existence. Shaw's representation
of their love is an outrage on history.

V

Shaw, it will be evident from our discussion, has taken sweeping
liberties with history and has given a personal interpretation of
Caesar. The immediate source of Shaw's *Caesar and Cleopatra*
is Mommsen's *History of Rome*. Mommsen was a German liberal,
disillusioned by the muddles and humiliations of the German
revolution of 1848-1849. Writing shortly after the revolution
he felt the need for a great man to bring order out of the chaos
created by the failure of the German people to realise its political
aspirations. He idealised Caesar to impress upon his countrymen
that a strong man was needed to save Germany from ruin.
Mommsen is a judicious historian but his account of Julius Caesar
is rather a panegyric and many of his statements are in contradiction to the classical as well as modern authorities. Shaw has
taken some hints from Mommsen, but in his representation
of Caesar as a man without worldly ambition and, especially,
in his treatment of the relation between Caesar and Cleopatra,
which is the main theme of the play, he has got from
Mommsen only slight hints, if hints they might be called, and has
idealised Caesar by exaggerating and, often, turning facts topsy-

turvy. This idealisation is the product of his professed purpose
to draw the picture of a superman from history just as Mommsen's
idealisation is the product of his yearning for a strong man to solve
the problems of Germany.

Shaw's Caesar is not a faithful portrait of a historical character,
but it does not matter. Shaw in this play has given a portrait of
a great man of his conception, a portait which, judged by the
consistency of the portraiture and the piquancy of its relationship
to general truth, is convincing. Compounded of an indomitable
will, an ability to influence other people and a capacity to accomplish
his purposes, Caesar is an extraordinary man; and he occupies a
very prominent place in the portrait-gallery of Shaw. He is a fine
realist, a sublime artistic creation, and it is immaterial that he is
not an exact replica of the Caesar of history.

Notes

1. Shaw's letter to Mrs. Mansfield, (Archibald Henderson, *Bernard Shaw:
    Playboy and Prophet*, p. 401).
2. *Advice to a Young Critic*, p. 77.
3. *Shaw and the Nineteenth Century Theatre*, p. 364.
4. A.C Ward, *Bernard Shaw*, p. 80.
5. St. John Ervine, *Bernard Shaw: His Life*, *Work and Friends*, p. 334.
6. Shaw's statement to Archibald Henderson (Archibald Henderson, *Bernard
    Shaw: Playboy and Prophet*, pp. 492–3).
7. G.K. Chesterton, *Bernard Shaw*, p. 152.
8. *The Art of Bernard Shaw*, p. 119.
9. *Plutarch's Lives*, translated by John and William Langhorne, p. 235.
10. Ibid., p. 272.
11. Gaius Suetonius Tranquiullus, *The Twelve Caesars*, translated by Robert
    Graves, p. 14.
12. Ibid., p. 41.
13. Will Durant, *The Story of Civilization*, vol., III, pp. 195–6.
14. G.K. Chesterton, op. cit., pp. 11–12.
15. *The Art of Bernard Shaw*, p. 118.
16. Theodor Mommsen, *The History of Rome*, abridged by C. Bryans and
    F.J.R. Hendy, vol. v, pp. 468–9.
17. *The Art of Bernard Shaw*, p. 118.
18. Theodor Mommsen, op. cit., p. 485.
19. Gaiuss Suetonius Tranquiullus, op. cit., p. 40.
20. Ibid., p. 38.
21. Will Durant, op. cit., vol. III, p. 187.
22. Preface to *Three Plays for Puritans*, p. 29.

23. Theodor Mommsen, op. cit., p. 307.
24. *The Twelve Caesars*, op. cit., p. 31.
25. Ibid., p. 31.
26. Will Durant, op. cit., p. 196.
27. Emil Ludwig, *Cleopatra, The Story of a Queen*, p. 33.
28. Ibid., p. 21.
29. *Plutarch's Lives*, Translated by John and William Langhorne, p. 266.
30. W.E. Heitland, *A Short History of the Roman Republic*, p. 465.

4. Saint Joan

I

Saint Joan, one of Shaw's masterpieces, was written when Shaw was at the ripe age of sixtyseven. Strange that Shaw, who had never cared to dramatise any character from hagiology, was drawn to this girl saint. Joan of Arc was canonised in 1920, and Mrs. Shaw was greatly impressed by this event. She suggested Joan as a subject to her husband. And though Shaw had never been particularly interested in Joan, he read the records of her trials made by Jules Quicherat and found them highly dramatic and decided to write a play about her.[1] He became deeply interested in the subject, because he 'must have realized that here was an opportunity to study and recreate a person who united in herself so much that he had divided between his practical and idealistic characters'.[2] He felt that he was inspired to write the play, and asserted that the play was written by Joan herself and that he had only arranged it for the stage.[3]

Saint Joan proved to be Shaw's most popular play. Some critics regard it as Shaw's best play, some as the greatest historical drama since Shakespeare. Even J.M. Robertson, who devoted a whole book to refuting Shaw's historicity, calls it a 'brilliant play'. *Saint Joan* is the work of a deeply religious man. But, it must be mentioned here, Shaw is a religious man not in the conventional sense of the term, but only in the sense that he believes in the primacy of the spirit and in Creative Evolution.

One is deeply stirred by the intensity of religious emotion of *Saint Joan*. This play, says Shaw, set up a standard which uplifted many young women 'beyond vulgarity and meanness' and having seen it, many schoolboys said that they 'could pray to St. Joan but not to Jesus Christ'.[4] Yet the play was banned in the United States on religious grounds and Shaw was described as 'a mocking Irishman' and his play as 'a satire against Church and State which are made to appear stupid and inept'.[5] The most talked of man of his time, Shaw was often misunderstood. He was profoundly religious but many regarded him as the devil's disciple. This confusion about him was mainly due to the fact that he irritated and repelled many by his seeming heresies, economic, political, moral and religious. In *Saint Joan* he has defended the judges who condemned Joan to death while posterity and popular judgement accused them of cozenage and declared the trial void on that account. This defence of the Ecclesiastical and Inquisitorial Courts offended the public taste which denounced Shaw as an irreligious man.

Shaw's religion is the religion of Creative Evolution which affirms the individual will as the true motive power in the world. A fundamental tenet of his religion of Creative Evolution is that the will must not be suppressed but freed, that a saintly deed consists not in immolating the self but in liberating the self. This doctrine is opposed to Catholicism which does not tolerate freethinking. Shaw looked upon Saint Joan as a vital genius, a great experiment of the Life Force, the Word made Flesh. But Catholicism which could not tolerate the claim of an individual to divine revelation found her guilty of offences against the Church which is the bride of Christ and the common morality of Christendom and excommunicated and handed her over to the secular power. Joan must obey her conscience, because conscience is the Voice of God; and the Roman Catholic Church must excommunicate her as a heretic and blasphemer, because it cannot admit private judgement as trustworthy interpreter of the Will of God without compromising its position and authority. Thus there is a conflict between private judgement in matters of faith and conduct and the established religion, and in this conflict Joan is crushed. This conflict is the essence of the drama.

Shaw, however, is not so much concerned with the particular tragedy of Joan as with the fate of all the vital geniuses in whom the Creative Will expresses itself in the form of celibacy and sainthood. Anybody who claims to have direct revelation cannot be accepted without enquiry by the Church as a Saint, for a lunatic or an impostor may make such a claim; but in ignoring such a claim the Church may mistake a saint for a lunatic or an impostor. The clash between an individual and the established religion in which a great experiment of the Life Force like a Jesus, or a Joan, or a Galileo is crushed has been going on since time immemorial, and this clash, according to Shaw, is the true tragedy of life. This is a great problem which is very difficult to solve. For, as A.C. Ward so nicely puts it, 'Liberty breeds Anarchy; Authority breeds Tyranny. The only way of escape from Anarchy is into Authority; the only cure for Tyranny is Liberty. This, to the end of time, is the human dilemma, the dilemma propounded in Saint Joan.'[6]

An ardent advocate of the humanist religion of Creative Evolution, Shaw is depressed by the spectacle of the tremendous obstacles that man in his short-sightedness puts in the way of the Will. Cauchon's cry in the Epilogue 'Must then a Christ perish in torment in every age to save those that have no imagination?' reveals the deep anguish of Shaw's heart. The sadness of Joan's 'Oh God that madest this beautiful earth, when will it be ready to receive Thy Saints? How long, O Lord, how long?' reveals a heart that bleeds to see the hostility of the world to a religion that can help man to rise higher and higher in the scale of evolution. As in other religious teachers, Shaw's optimism is sicklied over with a cast of sadness. Like Joan he too has a sense of spiritual isolation: 'I am alone on earth: I have always been alone.' But like Joan he does not despair: 'Do not think you can frighten me by telling me that I am alone. France is alone; and God is alone; and what is my loneliness before the loneliness of my country and my God? I see now that the loneliness of God is His strength: what would He be if He listened to your jealous little counsels? Well, my loneliness shall be my strength too; it is better to be alone with God: His friendship will not fail me, nor His counsel, nor His love. In his strength I will dare, and dare, and dare, until I die. I will go out now to the common people, and let the love in their eyes comfort me for the hate in yours. You will all be glad to see me burnt; but if I go through the fire I shall go through it to their hearts for ever and ever. And so, God be with me.' Great experiments of the Life Force, like Joan, are put to death by the world but they always win ultimate victory. Joan is burnt but her will survives with greater energy as a creative force. As she herself says, she goes through the fire and conquers the hearts of the people for ever. Even the most relentless of her accusers and persecutors, Chaplain de Stogumber, who is 'bloodthirsty' in his pursuit of heresy, is overwhelmed with remorse to see her tragedy. Her death is not the end, but the beginning of what she stands for. Warwick, in the Epilogue, aptly tells Joan, 'Your spirit conquered us, madam, in spite of our faggots.' The theme of *Saint Joan* is a vindication of the claims of Shaw's religion of Creative Evolution.[7] And it is the intense religious emotion of the play that makes it exalting. It is an elevating religious play stamped with all the insignia of superb craftsmanship.

II

Saint Joan is regarded as one of the greatest play of the twentieth century. Notwithstanding the importance of his thought and philosophy, Shaw's dramatic virtues deserve primary consideration, and it is in these virtues that the assurance of his survival lies. Shaw refused to write a single line for art's sake alone, and reiterated that it was never his ambition to be a dramatist in the accepted sense of the term. But what he could do along the old line he has shown in *Candida*. And *Saint Joan* clearly shows that if he had not cared so much to preach the doctrine of Creative Evolution, he might have written excellent conventional stage plays, and *did* write good plays, if not conventional ones.

In *Saint Joan* Shaw's dramatic instinct has fused the setting, action, dialogue, characterisation and plot with the dominant idea. The protagonist, Saint Joan, sees visions and hears voices commanding her to expel the English from France and establish the Dauphin on the French throne. She succeeds in doing both but is hampered by conflict with the combined power of the State and the Church. In the struggle that results from the conflict she stands alone. And the play turns upon the opposition between herself and her accusers. She puts her conscience against the established judgement of the Church even though her life is at stake. All the events that lead to the catastrophe are arranged in a sequential, logical pattern which shows the necessity governing human actions and gives universality to the story of an individual. Joan is captured and sold to the English, tried by the Ecclesiastical and Inquisitorial Courts, condemned and burnt. Every action in the play is directed towards this tragic catastrophe.

Although the theme is brilliantly conceived and the heroine and her antagonist are built in the heroic mould, the dramatic action has one serious flaw. In the first three scenes the movement of the play is derived from the movement of the people for national freedom with Joan at the helm. She has instilled enthusiasm, courage and determination into the hesitant and diffident people around her. Action begins at the end of the first scene when, after overcoming the opposition of de Boudricourt she dashes out wildly excited by her success followed by Poulengey. There is further movement at the end of the second scene when she gets the command of the army from the King and flashes out her sword and La Hire and all the knights follow her, shouting 'To Orleans'. The onward impetus of the movement is still further intensified at the end of the third scene when the wind suddenly changes and Joan and Dunois rush off to lead the French into battle and victory and the page 'capers out after them, and with excitement', shouting 'The Maid! God and the Maid! Hurray ay—ay!'

It will be evident that the French national movement with Joan at its helm constitutes the action of the first three scenes. In the fourth scene also the national movement is the mainspring of action, for here the Earl of Warwick and Peter Cauchon, the Bishop of Beauvais, decide to liquidate Joan because she preaches the heresy of nationalism which runs against the basic tenets of feudalism which is international. Even in the fifth scene the idea of the national movement is dominant. The crowning of the Dauphin as the King of France, Joan's desire to resume the war inspite of the opposition of the King, the Church and the General commanding the army are all vitally connected with the national movement. But here Shaw shifts his ground, for henceforth Joan is shown not so much as the leader of the people as a lonely saint seeing visions and hearing voices. The conflict is not between the leader of a national movement on the one side and the Church and the State on the other, but between an inspired saint believing in mystic experiences and those who do not believe in them. Then in the Trial Scene the national movement is entirely forgotten, and Joan is tried not as one who is guilty of nationalism but for the heresy of seeing visions and hearing voices.

Thus in the first four scenes of the play Shaw dramatises the French national movement and in the last two scenes he shifts his ground and dramatises what he states in the Preface: 'The conflict of the Regal, Sacerdotal, and Prophetic power, in which Joan was crushed.' As a result of this shifting of ground the role assigned to the Earl of Warwick comes to an abrupt end. Shaw has failed to show that the Church and the State combined in natural hatred to crush Joan. Dr. Sengupta rightly says: 'The conflict between Joan and Warwick has not, therefore, been effectively dramatised...and no wonder he [Warwick] fades into a shadowy and ineffective character.'[8]

Let us now turn to the characters. If, as Aristotle said, plot is the soul of the drama, character is its body. And no play can be truly great if its characters are not convincing. It is said that

Shaw has not a profound insight into human character, that his
characters are not plausibly motivated, that they are not sharply
individualised but are mere puppets to express their creator's
views. But these charges cannot be levelled against *Saint Joan*.
Here although all the characters are transcribed from history
Shaw has endowed them with originality and has given them
'in an uncommon degree that sense of belonging to a larger-
than-stage life which is essential to verisimilitude'.[9] The
characters do things required of them by the plot but they are
also interesting and complex enough in their own right to be
worth caring about. The Earl of Warwick is a perfect representative of the feudal aristocracy and English nationality, yet
he is far more than the lay figure he would have been were he
that alone; he is flesh and blood. Fearing that Joan might
undermine the feudal system by establishing her new nationalism
and making the King absolute autocrat, he gets her arrested and
hands her over to Cauchon, as is required by the plot; but Shaw
has given us a glimpse of his other interests which have nothing
to do with those with which the play is concerned. His preoccupation with the 'well-placed columns of rich black writing in
beautiful borders, and illuminated pictures cunningly inset' in a
'bonny book' in the English tent in the fourth scene reveals an
aspect of his life which is unconnected with feudal statecraft.

The Dauphin is a historical figure, weak, stupid, petulant and
ineffectual among his courtiers, but Shaw has made him an
admirable figure by putting into his mouth words he in real life
could never have found for himself:

Yes : it is always you good men that do the big mischief.
Look at me! I am not Charles the Good, nor Charles the
Wise, nor Charles the Bold. Joan's worshippers may even
call me Charles the Coward because I did not pull her out of
the fire. But I have done less harm than any of you. You
people with your heads in the sky spend all your time trying
to turn the world upside down; but I take the world as it is, and
say that top-side up is right side up; and I keep my nose pretty
close to the ground. And I ask you, what King of France has
done better, or been a better fellow in his little way?

Every character in *Saint Joan* contributes to the development of the action and has at the same time distinctive idiosyncrasies. Robert de Boudricourt, who helps Joan to proceed to the Dauphin, has no will of his own and like all will-less people he is self-assertive and loud-mouthed and disguises his defeat by bullying the weakling of a steward. Dunois, who surrenders his command to Joan and follows her to relieve besieged Orleans, lives a rough military life but is endowed with poetic sensibility which is seen in his invocation to the Kingfisher: 'Blue bird, blue bird, since I am friend to thee, change thou the wind for me'; and his mystic faith in divine miracles makes him surrender the command of the King's army to the Maid. It is a ruffianly English soldier, who fashions a rude cross for Joan; a bad man is not wholly bad.

Saint Joan is one of the outstanding individual characters in the portrait gallery of Shaw. She, like Candida, Major Barbara, Bluntschli and Father Keegan, is an unforgettable personality, for she has that individuality that lives in its own right. Shaw's Saint Joan is a combination of many contraries. She is a woman who puts on man's dress and delights in manly pursuits. Without training of any sort she becomes a military commander of almost incredible courage and strategic insight, worthy of comparison with Napoleon. She is a mystic who sees visions and hears voices and at the same time 'a thorough daughter of the soil in her peasant-like matter-of-factness and doggedness' and wins battles by hard-headed calculations. She is a professed and most pious Catholic Saint who 'acts as if she herself were the Church', thus defying a fundamental tenet of the Catholic Church which denies divine revelation to an individual, and preaches the theory of 'France for the Frenchmen', thus undermining the universality of feudal nobility. She has been identified with the Crown and the Church though the former abandoned her and the latter condemned her to death. She is a genius who does not know A from B and does not realise the nature of the forces arrayed against her. But she is a born boss compelling everybody, from her uncle to the King, to obey her commands, and her military talent puts to rout the well organised forces of England, but she is at length captured by the Burgundians and handed over to the Inquisition. She is harmed by the people she helps and hated by the people she loves. She is put to death to live for ever in the hearts of men. And her history begins with her execution. The combination of these contradictory qualities makes her 'a credible historical phenomenon' and a stage figure of living warmth. The burning of Joan is a stigma on human civilisation which posterity tried to wipe out by her canonisation. And her canonisation is a recognition of the supremacy of personal liberty in matters of religion.

Shaw's gift for dialogue and his ability to write long speeches also contribute largely to the dramatic effect of *Saint Joan*. The Shavian dialogue is marked by lucidity, vigorous force, conversationalism and musical cadence, and all this makes his dialogue 'far finer than the dialogue of any dramatist who has written in English in the past two-hundred years'.[10] And, as Allardyce Nicoll says, 'The range of his characters' utterances is always basically theatrical : its rhythms and its sentence patterns, of course, are characteristically his own, just as, let us say, Shakespeare's speech belongs to himself.'[11] As a typically Shavian conversation piece may be cited the verbal exchanges among Warwick, Stogumber and Cauchon in the fourth scene of *Saint Joan*. These three persons sit at a table and talk and talk and talk, and the audience or the readers remain spell-bound for about half an hour. Drama is literature of action while here are words, words, words. But this contributes to the development of the plot as much as scenes of action, for action need not always be external. The clash of attitudes in the dialogues between Warwick and Cauchon, intermittently disturbed by the all-too-simple patriotic views of Stogumber, forms the basis of the trial scene. The scene is a long conversation piece but it never flags. The opposition between Warwick and Cauchon reaches a climax when, arguing from different angles, they ultimately decide between them the fate of Joan in which everybody is intensely interested.

In Shaw's plays there are a number of passages of poetic beauty —Julius Caesar's apostrophe to the Sphinx, Lilith's soliloquy concluding *Back to Methuselah*, Dubedat's dying speech, Captain Shotover's short speech on the monotony of sea-life. But the largest number of such poetic passages is to be found in *Saint Joan*—Joan's reflections on solitude, her speech immediately after she tears up her recantation, the heart-rending words with which the Epilogue ends, and several others. Then there are in this play many passages which for their oratorical and dialectical skill, verbal beauty, brilliance, wisdom and effectiveness have become classic. The Inquisitor's oration on heresy,

Cauchon's speech that follows immediately, and the latter's defence of the wisdom and knowledge of the Church are three such passages. All these passages add to the total effect of the play and have their share in making it Shaw's most popular play.

It will be evident from our discussion that *Saint Joan* is a fine piece of dramatic art. But its Epilogue has been the subject of acute literary controversy. Critics on both sides of the Atlantic have unanimously decried its inclusion and have suggested that by its excision the play could be shortened and improved. But Shaw took no more notice of them 'than Einstein of the people who are incapable of Mathematics'. He defended its inclusion by saying that the canonisation of Joan was more important than her incineration and he could not stultify himself, as he says in the Preface, by ending the play with Joan's execution since her history in the world began rather than ended with her execution.

The Epilogue undoubtedly detracts from the dramatic effect of the play. The concluding part of the sixth scene is one of the most impressive dramatic situations in all Shaw's work. Joan has been taken away to the stake, and in the courtyard 'the glow and flicker of fire can now be seen reddening the May daylight'. The Inquisitor and Cauchon take leave of Warwick and with a heavy heart proceed towards the stake. Warwick, who is eager to see that everything is soon over, is left alone in oppression, silence and loneliness. He longs for some companion.

WARWICK: Hallo: some attendance here! (*Silence*). Hallo, there! (*Silence*). Hallo! Brian, you young blackguard, where are you? (*Silence*). Guard! (*Silence*). They all have gone to see the burning : even that child.

All, 'even that child', have gone to the stake. Joan who had been deserted by the people has again become the leader of the people.

The silence is soon broken by the Chaplain who staggers in, frantically howling and sobbing, and saying, 'She cried to Thee in the midst of it : Jesus ! Jesus ! Jesus ! She is in Thy bosom; and I am in hell for evermore.'

Shortly the Executioner comes and says, 'Her heart would not burn, my lord; but everything that was left is at the bottom of the river. You have heard the last of her.' Warwick responds with wise caution : 'The last of her? Hm! I wonder.' The play should

end here. Nothing further about her future needs to be told.
She has won by her death what she struggled for in life.

The Epilogue, as Allardyce Nicoll says, is 'not an integral part
of the play'.[12] Nor is it a representation of an actual happening,
but it is in perfect accord with the spirit of history, and it is for
the spirit of history, and not for actual happening, that Shaw
cared. Joan's canonisation is a belated recognition of the ultimate
triumph of the Life Force of which Joan is the highest exempli-
fication, and is a vindication of the claims of Shaw's religion of
Creative Evolution. Shaw has always a message to convey,
and without the Epilogue the play would have been a sensational
tale of a girl who liberated her country from the foreigners by
fighting valiantly and was at length burnt as a heretic by the
people for whom she fought. The Epilogue shows how mankind
has expiated its mistake in burning a real saint as a heretic. It
gives us a vision of life that is hopeful, and without it we would
have despaired of humanity.

Apart from the message it conveys the Epilogue stands apart
as something austere and august. Even if we deny its dramatic
propriety we cannot ignore its beauty and grandeur. Without
the Epilogue we would have lost the superb litany of praise by
Cauchon, Dunois, the Archbishop, Warwick, De Stogumber,
the Inquisitor, the soldier, the Executioner and Charles succes-
sively, the 'lovely wisdom' of Cauchon's anguished cry, 'must
then a Christ perish in torment in every age to save those that
have no imagination?' and the heart touching final words of
Joan that end the Epilogue. The Epilogue is one of the most
moving and impressive scenes Shaw ever wrote.

III

The first and the second sections of this chapter have been devoted
to a discussion of the theme and the dramatic qualities respectively
of *Saint Joan*. Let us now enquire into the historicity of the
play and the Preface, taken together, which is the main purpose
of the present study. As his way is, Shaw says in the Preface
that *Saint Joan* is utterly historical. And to emphasise this he
asserts that it was written by Joan herself: 'I have done nothing
but arranged her for the stage. There really was such a woman.

She did and said all those things. Make your offerings at her altar, not at mine.'[13]

But Shaw's claim of historicity has been hotly challenged by a number of critics. Foremost among them is J.M. Robertson who in his *Mr. Shaw and the Maid* says that Shaw 'has falsified the record of the trial' and invented a 'neo-Irish Joan', 'a doctrinaire figure which has no historic reality'. Shaw's picture, according to Robertson, is 'an express falsification of the history', and his drama 'a pseudo-historic drama'. Desmond MacCarthy says that the atmosphere of the play 'is not that of the Middle Ages' and that the play 'is full of spiritual anachronisms'.[14] David Daiches holds the view that Shaw interprets the past in terms of his own contemporary society and his Saint Joan is a Shavian heroine rather than a convincing historical character.[15] Dr. Sengupta's view is that the picture of Joan 'is not in all respects true to history'.[16] C.B. Purdom says, 'Although Shaw scrupulously based himself upon the documents, it may be admitted that his account of the trial is not literally correct, without, however, reducing the truth of his drama.'[17] G.G. Coulton, an eminent authority on medieval history, admires the play but dismisses the Preface as childish.[18] And he is of the opinion that Joan did not get a fair trial.[19]

But there are others who support Shaw's claim. Archibald Henderson says that *Shaw's Saint Joan* is 'amazingly close to historic fact'.[20] St. John Ervine is inclined to believe that Shaw's picture of the Maid is historically true. While defending Shaw against the charge of G.G. Coulton he says, 'G.B.S. consulted the documents in Joan's history and came to conclusions that seem infantile to Coulton; but who will dare to say that the vision of a man of genius is less authoritative than the recordings of confidential clerks?'[21] Desmond MacCarthy, though he does not find the atmosphere of the Middle Ages in this play, is of the opinion that Shaw 'is careful of historic facts in this play'.[22] A historian of the eminence of Charles Wayland Lightbody in *The Judgements of Joan*, which forms part of a large research project, describes Shaw's play as a 'notable work'.[23]

Shaw's view of Saint Joan, it will be evident, has been denounced by eminent critics and historians, and equally eminent critics and historians have upheld his view. A study of Joan, indeed, is beset with innumerable difficulties, and it is wellnigh impossible to see her in proper perspective and arrive at a view that will be final. Joan has fascinated all kinds of writers—historians, biographers, playwrights, poets, philosophers—but their approaches to her have been infinitely varied. The Catholics and Protestants, the radical nationalists and reactionary chauvinists, the realists and the romanticists are sharply divided in their opinion about her. She has been variously described as a genius, a saint, a virago, an impostor, a trafficker in witchcraft, a devil, a puppet of designing men. Equally strong arguments have been put forth by her accusers and defenders, all basing their arguments on the proceedings of the trials. But the proceedings admit of various interpretations and are a source of intense 'psychological conflict'.

In dealing with Joan historians and artists have often been too much influenced by personal passions and prejudices, by doctrinaire approaches, by the climate of opinion of their respective ages. The artist has his own difficulties with materials so complex and controversial. He cannot take liberties with the material, nor can he ignore contemporary taste and expectations. He has to make his subject come to life in its own environment and reveal its inner meanings to modern tastes. But Shaw claims to have given us in his play 'all that need be known about her'; but 'as it is for the stage use I had to condense into three and a half hours a series of events which in their historical happening were spread over four times as many months'. Shaw says that it is the *a priori* assumption of the writers on Joan that it is the conflict of villain and heroine in Joan's history that is responsible for falsifying the whole picture. One sterling quality of Shaw is that he can maintain a perfect balance between opposing views. He knows that it is wrong to suppose that in a quarrel one party is always right and the other always wrong; more often both the parties are equally right and equally wrong. The realisation of this fundamental fact has enabled him to study the history of Joan in true perspective. Most of the writers on Joan have taken for granted that if she were right, those who opposed her were wrong; or if she were wrong, those who opposed her were right. Shaw shows that Joan was right and also those who condemned her to death were right. Eric Bentley aptly says, 'In *Saint Joan* the happy fact about his impartiality is that he seems to be, not on neither side (like, say, Galsworthy in *Strife*) but on both sides.'[24]

To see the history of Joan in proper perspective it is necessary to have a clear idea of the political condition of France during her time—the condition which formed the background of her career and its motivating force. France was divided into two political parties—the Armagnacs and the Burgundians. The Armagnacs were the followers of Charles VII who was debarred from succession for various reasons and the Burgundians were the followers of the Duke of Burgundy, Philip the Good who was in alliance with England. Overcoming all opposition offered by the Duke of Burgundy, Joan crowned the Dauphin Charles in the Cathedral of Rheims. She roused the patriotism of the nation and undermined the English domination. The Burgundians looked upon her as the child of the very Devil, a witch, or at best a brazen impostor, doing the Devil's work by helping the vicious Armagnacs. In the fifteenth century there were the chronicles of the Armagnac party which were all in praise of Joan and there were the chronicles of the Burgundian party all condemnatory of her. Thus the contemporary source-materials relating to Joan fall sharply into two main groups, one group consisting of the Armagnac chronicles and the record of the Rehabilitation, and the other group consisting of the Burgundian chronicles and the record of the original trial. As all later accounts of Joan are based on these two groups of antagonistic materials her history has become a history of contradictory judgements, and the real Joan has been quite lost to view beneath 'the successive coats of grime and whitewash, war-paint and plaster of paris sanctity'. Shakespeare's portrait of Joan in *Henry IV, Part I,* for instance, is vitiated by Burgundian prejudice. Shaw steered clear of the varied approaches based on two party lines during five centuries and scrupulously based himself upon the records of the two trials unearthed by Jules Quicherat and gave a picture of Joan which is essentially correct.

IV

Shaw, in the play and the Preface, does not depart from historical truth in any essential particular although he does not represent historical events exactly as they occurred but fits them into the limits of time and space by a process of condensation which is permissible to art. All the characters in the play are historical

—Joan, Charles, Warwick, Peter Cauchon, Dunois, La Hire,
Robert de Boudricourt, Stogumber, Courcelles, Giles de Rais,
Promoter D' Estivet, Inquisitor Brother John Lemaiter, the
Executioner; and they all acted and behaved in the manner as
Shaw represents them.

Shaw's portrayal of Joan's career and his representation of a
number of incidents of her life with their dates and the names of
the people concerned are authentic. The daughter of a headman
of the village of Domremy, Joan could neither read nor write but
was a born leader with a craze for soldiery and the rough life,
compelling everybody to obey her commands. She compelled
her uncle to take her to the Squire of Boudricourt who, though at
first adamant in his refusal to her demands, was so impressed
by her that he gave her a guard of men, armour and horse and
she went off to the Dauphin at Chinon. She at once recognised
the Dauphin who had hidden himself in a crowd of courtiers, and
the Dauphin gave her the command of the army at Orleans. At
Orleans the army needed a west wind to enable it to cross the
Loire. Joan prayed to St. Catherine and at once the wind changed,
and she rushed off to lead the army into battle and victory. She
then crowned the Dauphin in the Cathedral at Rheims. Then
she planned to take Paris but could not because Charles, who
hoped to 'make a good treaty with the Duke of Burgundy' thwar-
ted her plan. Then followed a bleak period when she was deserted
by most of her comrades in arms, captured at Compiegne by the
Burgundians, tried by the Ecclesiastical and Inquisitorial Courts
and burnt at the stake.

The other incidents and events of Joan's life and career dealt
with by Shaw in the play and the Preface are also authentic. Joan,
while still a child, wanted to run away from home and be a soldier,
and for this her father and brothers threatened to drown her in
the river. In her expedition against the English she was helped
most by Jack Dunois who surrendered his command to Joan and
blindly followed her to relieve beleaguered Orleans and La Hire
who fell under her influence to such an extent that he abandoned
his long habit of swearing. Her prediction that the English
Captain, William Glasdale, who blasphemously insulted her
would die a drowning death came true. She possessed the mystic
sword she had found in the Church of St. Catherine. While in
prison she once fell ill after eating a carp. As she climbed a

scaling ladder at the bridge-head of Orleans, her throat was
pierced through by an English arrow. While a captive she tried
to escape from Beaurevoir Castle by jumping from a tower sixty
feet high. Joan, as she frankly told her judges, did not tell the
whole truth, for sometimes a man is hanged for telling the truth.
During her trial she was induced to recant and sign a confession
that her voices were temptations by demons, but when she was
condemned to lifelong imprisonment she withdrew her recantation.
From the pyre she asked for a cross and an English soldier gave
her a little cross made of two little sticks tied together and she
died embracing it and uttering the name of Jesus. Her heart
could not be burnt, and all that remained and the ashes were
thrown into the river. Some of the ecclesiastical judges who had
sent her to the stake as a witch were maddened with remorse and
wept bitterly when they realised that they had burnt a saint. She
had the certain fore-knowledge that she would 'last only a year'.
For her service to the nation she asked nothing for herself except
that her native village, Domremy, should be exempt from taxation,
and her request was granted.

But mere reproduction of facts and incidents from Joan's life,
however accurate, is not enough. What is needed is an effort
of the historical imagination in order to enter into the atmosphere
of the fifteenth century. But to leap over five and a half centuries
is not an easy task. And critics like Desmond MacCarthy and
David Daiches have found fault with Shaw, because 'the play
does not recall the atmosphere of the Middle Ages' and because
'Shaw interprets historical characters in the light of his own modern
understanding and preoccupations'. On the other hand, Shaw,
in the Preface, blames Shakespeare, because 'there is not a breath
of medieval atmosphere in Shakespeare's histories', and he asserts:

> Nature abhors a vacuum in Shakespeare; and I have taken
> care to let the medieval atmosphere blow through my play
> freely. Those who see it performed will not mistake the start-
> ling   event   it   records   for   a   mere   personal   accident.
> They will have before them not only the visible and human
> puppets, but the Church, the Inquisition, the Feudal System,
> with divine inspiration always beating against their too elastic
> limits: All more terrible in their dramatic force than any of the
> little mortal figures clanking about in plate armour or moving

silently in the frocks and hoods of the order of St. Dominic.

Let us now see whether Shaw's portrait of Saint Joan fits into the medieval background. The Middle Ages stand upon a foundation of credulity; it had implicit faith in the Church, the Inquisition and the Feudal System. Shaw suggests the credulity of the age by a number of miracles—the hens 'laying like mad', Joan's recognition of the Dauphin from a crowd of nobles, the change of the wind on the Loire, the drowning of Glasdale who had blasphemously insulted her, her jump from a tower sixty feet high without receiving any fatal injury, the fire that did not consume her heart. The position of the Church, the Inquisition and the feudal system is made clear through the speeches of Bishop Cauchon, Inquisitor Lemaiter and the Earl of Warwick respectively. Shaw's Joan shares the religious, social and moral attitudes of her time. However, the critics say, the effect of all this 'is neutralised by his [Shaw's] peculiar dramatic method of making each character speak with a self-conscious awareness of the orientation of his own point of view, which is utterly foreign to the times'.[25] Shaw himself admits that he has given to the age of Joan the immediacy and familiarity of the present and has interpreted history in modern terms so that it may be perfectly clear to a modern audience. And, as has already been pointed out in chapter one, seeing the past through eyes accustomed to the writer's age and, consequently, in seeing it in reference to that which seems familiar are not distorted interpretations of history as is supposed by some critics of Shaw. The contention of the critics that Shaw is historically wrong in interpreting Joan's age in terms of the present is based on a misconception of the method of history and the nature of historical truth.

Shaw's picture of Saint Joan and the age she belongd to, it will be evident from our discussion, is historically authentic. There is even a close resemblance between the speeches in the play, especially those of Joan, and the corresponding Records of the two trials, which shows that Shaw has not only read the Records minutely but has also taken scrupulous care not to distort any facts in any way. Archibald Henderson aptly says that 'this play is more likely a puzzle by its conflict with current fictions about Saint Joan than by its adaptation of facts to the stage'.[26] Shaw finds such fictions in the works of, among others, Shakespeare,

Anatole France and Andrew Lang and accuses them of having
distorted the picture of the Maid and the fifteenth century beyond
recognition. An examination of these criticisms will show that
Shaw is right and the others are wrong.

Shakespeare, in *Henry VI, Part One*, has taken flagrant liberties
with Joan. He is an exponent of the 'English Theory' — the
theory that was derived from the Burgundian chronicles, that
Joan was a witch and strumpet, justly condemned. Shakespeare's
Joan appeals to the Duke of Burgundy as his 'humble handmaid'
and bewitches him with her words. She is presented as calling
upon the 'familiar spirits that are cull'd out of the powerful regions
under the earth' and she promises 'my body shall pay recompense
if you will grant my suit' and admits too late that they had deceived
her. When she is condemned to burn and when her appeals
fall flat on the ears of the English, she says:

> Will nothing turn your unrelenting hearts?
> Then, Joan, discover thine infirmity,
> That warranteth by law to be thy privilege—
> I am with child, ye bloody homicides:
> Murder not, then, the fruit within my womb,
> Although ye hale me to a violent death.

All this is, to say the least, blasphemy against one who, as has
already been shown, died by embracing an improvised cross and
uttering the name of Jesus. Rightly does Bullough call it 'a
fantasia on historical themes'.[27]

Anatole France has divested Joan of her extraordinary gifts—
her military talent, her mental strength, and her physical hardihood
—and represented her as a puppet, used as mascot by designing
clerics and generals to win victories by exploiting the superstitious
credulity of the age of faith. He says that 'if she moved multitudes
it was by the spreading abroad of countless legends which sprang
up wherever she went and made way before her. And indeed,
there is much food for thought in that dazzling obscurity which
from the very first enwrapped the Maid, in those radiant clouds of
myth, which, while concealing her, rendered her all the more
imposing.'[28] This, surely, is not a correct picture of the Maid
of France who, we learn from the two trial Records, rode long

distances on horseback, compelled her uncle, Robert de Boudricourt, and the Dauphin to do her will, led the dispirited and
panic-stricken French army into battle and victory, boldly
withstood a long trial and baffled the wits of her learned judges,
and suffered martyrdom claiming that her conduct was a matter
between God and herself instead of surrendering to affectionate
appeals or threats of torture. She was no puppet in the hands of
clerics and generals, as Anatole France suggests, but a person of
strong nerves, high intelligence, tenacious and dauntless will and
ever 'so positive', as Shaw says.

Andrew Lang wrote *The Maid of France* 'in a white heat of
indignation', in the hope of correcting 'grave errors' by showing
the iniquity of Joan's condemnation. He represents Peter Cauchon,
Bishop of Beauvais, as Joan's personal enemy, who travelled
'to Beaurevoir, to Compiegne, to Flanders, to the Duke of
Burgundy, in full fury for her blood', putting to her questions which
were 'purposely mixed and confused so as to entrap the Maid in
contradictions', prepared the Articles of accusation which were
'falsely extracted and unjustly composed' and thus condemning
her to the stake. The other judges are accused of complicity, and
the trial is declared to be unjust and unfair. That Andrew Lang
is entirely wrong will be evident from the discussion in the next
section which is devoted to an examination of the trial of Joan.

V

The trial of Joan, which has been described as 'a trial that has
become second in importance only to the trial of Christ', raised a
heated controversy which remains very much alive today, and
will perhaps never settle. More than three thousand books have
been written on Joan, and each of these books, far from settling
the problem, has added to the controversy. 'The more we study
Joan, the more in some respects, does she become an enigma.
She has the charm of an enigma, of a sphinx whose riddle many
of the greatest minds of more than five centuries have tried to
read.'[29]

Shaw claims, as his oculist friend reminded him, that his vision
is normal, for he sees things differently from and better than
other people. His unconventional outlook and originality are
best exemplified in his attitude towards the trial of Joan. The

trial at Rouen which had been held up to public execration for centuries, is represented by Shaw as a perfectly just and legal one. The judges who were condemned as corrupt, treachrous, lawless and infamous are shown to be honest, conscientious and righteous persons, treating Joan with special consideration, trying their utmost to release her from the peril she was obdurately floundering in, and at length condemning her strictly according to law. Thus, Shaw deviates from the practice of his predecessors in drama and biography and vindicates the Rouen trial and the judges who condemned her.

Now let us enquire into the trial and see whether Shaw's view of it can be upheld. Lord Acton describes the principle of the Inquisition as 'murderous'.[30] Indeed, Joan 'was tried under a system which is now universally held to be barbaric and unjust, but which was in her time, and for that matter, for centuries afterward, in full operation in every ecclesiastical court'.[31] Medieval conceptions of justice were different from modern conceptions of it. Joan was judicially burnt for crimes which today are not punishable. Indeed, the modern mind revolts against the idea of burning anybody alive, however grave the offence. Modern prejudices and biases may naturally stand in the way of our seeing the trial in true perspective. Hence for a proper appraisal of Joan's trial and the judgment passed upon her, it is necessary to guard against such subjectivity and make all allowance for the spirit of the Middle Ages and admit the general justice of inquisitorial law and procedure prevailing then.

Joan was arrested on suspicion of witchcraft and heresy and was surrendered to the spiritual jurisdiction of Pierre Cauchon, the Bishop of Beauvais, who was authorised by the University of Paris to hold an enquiry into her actions and sayings according to ecclesiastical laws. Cauchon, with his assistants, was engaged in a Preparatory Process, as it was called, from 9 January to 25 March.[32] The Preparatory Trial was followed by an Ordinary Trial which drew up seventy Articles of Accusation.[33] Next an epitome, in the form of twelve propositions, was prepared from this elaborate indictment and it was submitted to doctors and other men learned in canon and civil law, for their advice and consultation. They voted that Joan should be tenderly exhorted to submit and that the judgment of the University of Paris should be invoked. Accordingly on 18 April, the judges, with 'many men of honesty and learning, doctors and others', visited her prison and admonished and exhorted her to submit to the Church Militant, but to no purpose.[34] They reproved her again on 2 May, this time publicly, but in vain.[35] On 9 May, she was taken to the torture chamber, threatened with torture and was actually shown the rack but she remained as obdurate as before. However, the judges, 'fearing that the torments of torture would be of little profit to her, decided to postpone their application until they had received more complete advice on the subject'.[36] On 12 May, the judges met and concluded that it was neither necessary nor expedient to submit her to torture.[37] They then invoked the decisions of the University of Paris. The University of Paris found her guilty but asked the Rouen Tribunal to rebuke her once more and in the event of further contumacy to hand her over to the secular arm for due punishment.[38] Accordingly, on 23 May, Pierre Maurice, Canon of Rouen and a celebrated doctor of theology, read and explained to her the twelve articles, warned her of the danger she was floundering about in, and fervently begged her to submit to the Church, but Joan would not.[39] Next day, 24 May, was set for pronouncing the sentence. The preacher, Erard, a distinguished doctor of sacred theology, delivered his sermon and exhorted her to submit to Our Holy Mother Church all her words and deeds, but as she would not, Cauchon began to pronounce the sentence of death. Joan suddenly cried out that she would submit to the Church. Immediately Erard read the formula of abjuration which she repeated after him and signed.[40] Cauchon then read the mitigated sentence condemning her 'for salutary penance to perpetual imprisonment, with the bread of sorrow and water of affliction, that you may weep for your faults and never henceforth commit anything to occasion weeping'.[41] In four days she relapsed, and when on 28 May, the judges visited her in her prison they found her in man's dress. She told them that she had recanted 'only for fear of the fire', that God had sent her word through St. Catherine and St. Margaret, that 'she had done a great evil in declaring that what she had done was wrong'. She added 'she would rather do penance once and for all, that is die, than endure any longer the suffering of prison', that 'if the judges wished, she would once more wear woman's dress, but for the rest she would do no more'.[42] On 29 May, the judges met and decided to proceed against her as relapsed and on 30 May, the final sentence was pronounced and that very day she was burnt in the marketplace of Rouen.

From this outline of the trial, it will be evident that Shaw in his play has not taken any liberty with his source materials—the documents of the trial. But a number of critics have denounced the Preface where Shaw has put forth elaborate arguments to prove that the trial was perfectly legal and the judges perfectly righteous and conscientious. An examination of the contentions of the critics, biographers and historians will be necessary in order to estimate the worth and validity of Shaw's argument.

One allegation against the trial is that it was manipulated by English pressure and coercion. It is true that the English were the bitterest enemies of Joan, and they were glad to get rid of her. The Trial was financed by them and the outcome was pleasing to them. But it was not the English who conceived the idea of a Church trial of Joan; the idea originated with the University of Paris.[43] No doubt, as is alleged, the University of Paris was sympathetic with the English, but, as we shall see, there is no reason to believe so. It must be noted here that the University of Paris was then 'at the very height of its medieval fame and influence as a theological authority' and it 'occupied a highly privileged and independent position'.[44] Its letters[45] to the Duke of Burgundy, to Jean Luxembourg, to the King of France and England, insisting on the surrender of Joan to the Inquisitor or the Bishop of Beauvais clearly show that, in its decision to have a Church Trial of Joan, it acted independently of any English influence. The University pursued Joan with the conviction that she was a menace to the Church and it reproached the King, Henry VI, for delaying to bring her to trial, humbly beseeching him 'to avoid the reputation of negligence in so favourable and essential a matter'. It also reproached Cauchon for dilatoriness. It wanted to expedite the trial, for 'the length and delays are perilous, and a great and noble reparation is necessary to bring the people so scandalised by this woman, back to a true and holy doctrine and belief'. It sincerely believed her to be a heretic and tried to save the people from her clutches. It would punish her as a heretic but give her a chance to return to the way of truth and salvation. It sent a unanimous corroboration of the twelve articles drawn by the Rouen judges but asked them to reprehend her once again before excommunicating her and handing her over to the secular power.[46]

All this clearly shows that the University of Paris had been impartial. Above all, it, especially the Faculty of theology and the Faculty of Decrees, had many doctors and masters who were supreme authorities on law and theology throughout Christendom. To say that they all acted partially would be a flat contradiction of the evidence which proves that the prosecutors and the judges acted as scrupulously as learned people in the Middle Ages would be expected to do in a religious trial.

Another allegation is that the judges who tried Joan were self-seeking and corrupt men. It is alleged that Joan was responsible for driving Cauchon, the mainspring of the whole procedure, from his diocese a year before, and, therefore, he had private reasons for hostility to her and hence became an easy tool in the hands of the English. It is also alleged that the archiepiscopal seat of Rouen was specially procured for him because he had no jurisdiction there. It is true that she was responsible for driving him out from his cathedral, but this fact itself is not enough to prove that Cauchon was hostile to Joan. Cauchon's own claim to power and authority to act in the case was based on the fact that Joan was taken prisoner in his diocese of Beauvais.[47] A letter from the venerable chapter of the Cathedral of Rouen granted him territory during the vacancy of the archiepiscopel seat.[48] His appointment to conduct the trial of Joan was, therefore, quite proper and perfectly legal.

Bishop Cauchon was a man of rare intelligence and ability and thorough legal and theological training. He was, as a letter of the University of Paris says, 'a true pastor', who never 'displayed indifference when this celebrated work of exalting the divine name is in question, or the integrity and glory of the orthodox faith, and the salutary edification of the faithful people'.[49] He was full of 'pious concern for the public safety', and was always 'animated by an immense fervour of most singular charity'. In Joan's case he was determined to 'proceed in such a way that by God's help the matter should be conducted to the praise of our Lord and to the exaltation of the faith, so that our trial might be without flaw'.[50] There are ample instances to show that, notwithstanding his Anglo-Burgundian sympathies, he was never a tool of the English. It must be credited to the mercy of Cauchon that Joan was spared the customary torture, though she was threatened with it and shown the rack.[51] That his purpose was to bring her back to the way of truth and save the people from the pernicious influence of a heretic, as he sincerely believed her to be, is evident from the number of times he reproached Joan and exhorted her to surrender to the Church Militant. And the fact that he sought the opinions of all the doctors present in Rouen as well as the opinion of the University of Paris reveals his anxiety to guard against any miscarriage of justice. Cauchon's good faith and immunity from English influence are amply vindicated by one more incident. When, after her abjuration, Cauchon admitted Joan to penance, the English who had assembled to see her burned became furious and hurled stones at him and threatened him with swords, saying he had ill earned the money spent on him, but he defied and silenced them with a stern gesture.[52] An English ecclesiastic accused him of favouring her, and Cauchon turned on him with the words, 'You lie. It is my duty and profession to seek the salvation of her soul and body.'[53] Cauchon, as Shaw says, was a conscientious, capable and eloquent exponent of the Church Militant and the Church Litigant. And the Universal execration he has been subjected to is unjustified. Charles Wayland Lightbody justly says, 'It is one of the ironies of history that this man should have gone down alike in popular and in literary tradition as one of the blackest villains of all recorded time, worthy of comparison only with Pontius Pilate, because of his leading part in the trial of the peasant maid from Lorraine. whom, we must believe, he regarded sincerely as a heretic and a witch, a poisoned sheep which it was a matter of Christian duty to remove before it tainted the whole flock.'[54]

As regards the other judges, assessors and theologians and canonists of the University of Paris, suffice it to quote what Gilles, Lord Abbot of Ste. Trinité de Fecamp, said: 'Such men, in so great numbers, cannot be found in the whole world.'[55]

Another allegation is that Joan's demand at the beginning of the trial for a panel of judges in equal number from both the contending parties was refused. As G.G. Coulton says, this request 'had naturally enough been refused, it was not thus that the Inquisition worked, nor, except on the rare occasions, did any Bishop's Court'.[56] Shaw's explanation is also convincing: 'This is a valid objection to all such Tribunals; but in the absence of Neutral Tribunals they are unavoidable. A trial by Joan's French partisans would have been as unfair as a trial by her French opponents; and an equally mixed Tribunal would have produced a deadlock.'[57] We must also take note of the fact that later during the trial Joan herself had lost faith in the members of her own party. Asked by her judges whether she would refer the story of the crown to the Archbishop of Rheims or to other members of her party, she refused.[58] She also refused to submit her claims 'concerning the apparitions and all that was contained in the trial' to the judgment of 'three or four clergy of her own party'.[59] She also refused to 'refer herself to the Church of Poitiers where she was examined', saying, 'Do you think you will catch me in that way and draw me to you so?'[60] All that clearly emerges is that even the clergy of the Armagnac party had lost their faith in Joan and the presence of an equal number of judges from her party in the Tribunal would have made no substantial difference in the judgment.

Some critics are of the opinion that Joan's appeal that her case should be submitted to the Pope should have been granted. This opinion cannot be upheld. The ecclesiastical court and the Inquisition were specially created for the purpose of dealing with persons accused of heresy or witchcraft. Conceding to her appeal would have obliged the Ecclesiastical and Inquisitorial judges to concede to the appeals of others in similar situations. And it would have been impossible for the Pope to hear anybody who claimed innocence in such matters.

Throughout the trial Joan showed extreme obstinacy, and her conduct was often insulting to the judges, who, however, showed admirable patience and compassion. Asked if God had asked her to wear men's dress, she answered that 'dress was a small, nay, the least thing', and she added that she had taken man's dress at God's commands.[61] When they told her that she had abandoned her womanly commitments by wearing male attire, she said that there were plenty of other women 'to don them'. When Bishop Cauchon forbade her to leave the prison in the castle of Rouen without their authorisation under penalty of the crime of heresy, she replied that 'she did not accept this prohibition, adding that if she escaped, none could accuse her of breaking or violating her oath, since she had given her oath to none'. She further said, 'It is true that I wished and still wish to escape, as is lawful for any captive or prisoner.'[62] She often said, 'You will not know everything', 'I would rather have my head cut off than

tell you everything', 'You will not learn any more', 'I will not give
any further answer for the present'. She repeatedly refused to
take the prescribed oath, to repeat the Lord's prayer, and almost
every time she was requested to swear she gave a sharp retort.
When first exhorted to speak the truth, she answered, 'I do not
know what you wish to examine me on. Perhaps, you might ask
such things that I would not tell.'[63]   On 22 February, when she
was exhorted to answer truly, she said, 'You may well ask me
such things, that to some I shall answer truly, and to others I
shall not.'[64]   On 24 February, when the judges admonished her
thrice to speak the simple and absolute truth and to make no
reservation to her oath, she refused saying, 'By my faith, you could
ask things such as I would not answer.' She added, 'Perhaps
I shall not answer you truly in many things that you may ask me,
concerning the revelations; for perhaps you would constrain
me to tell things I have sworn not to utter, and so I should be
perjured, and you would not want that.'[65]   She further said that
there was a saying among little children, 'Men are sometimes hanged
for telling the truth.'[66]   Such answers which clearly indicate that
she was scornful of the precepts and sanctions of the Church and
was presumptuous in the extreme are plentifully found in the
Record.[67]   It may be mentioned here that 'none, not even a prince,
could refuse to take oath when required in matter of faith'.[68]   As
G.G. Coulton says, 'Joan's refusal to swear was heretical', and
'by plain Inquisitorial law she deserved the stake'.[69]

Yet her judges repeatedly pointed out her error, and remonstrated
with her to accept the Church instead of setting up her own private
judgement against it and claiming that her conduct was a matter
between God and herself. The three page appeal of Pierre
Maurice made on 23 May is worth quoting, but for want of space
only portions of it are given here:

Jeanne, dearest friend, it is now time, near the end of your trial
to think well over all that has been said. Although you have
four times already, by the Lord Bishop of Beauvais, by the
Lord Vicar of the Inquisitor...been most diligently admonished for the honour and reverence of God...up till now
you have not wished to listen....We should beg, exhort and
adivse you by the bowels of Our Lord Jesus Christ who suffered
cruel death for the redemption of mankind, to correct your

words and submit them to the judgement of the Church, as every loyal Christian is bound and obliged to do. Do not permit yourself to be separated from Our Lord who created you to be a partaker of His glory....Suppose your king had appointed you to defend a fortress, forbidding you to let anyone enter. Would you not refuse to admit whoever claimed to come in his name but brought no letter or authentic sign? Likewise Our Lord Jesus Christ, when He ascended into Heaven, committed the government of his Church to the apostle St. Peter and his successors, forbidding them to receive in the future those who claimed to come in His name but brought no other token than their own words. Cease, I pray you, from uttering these things if you love your Creator....Obey the Church and submit to its judgement; know that if you do not, if you persevere in this error, your soul will be condemned to eternal punishment and perpetual torture.... Let no human pride and empty shame, which perhaps constrain you, hold you back....On behalf of your judges the Lord Bishop of Beauvais and the Lord Vicar of the Inquisitor, I admonish, beg and exhort. ...From these ills may Our Lord preserve you![70]

There can be little doubt about the deep sincerity and good faith of the judges. Their threat of torture, their repeated admonitions and exhortation, and their appeals were of no avail. Inspite of the repeated efforts of her judges she was adamant in what they had every right to regard as her heresy. The Church had no alternative but to excommunicate her and hand her over to the secular arm to be burnt. For, as Bishop Cauchon, in Shaw's play, says,

What will the world be like when the Church's accumulated wisdom and knowledge and experience, its councils of learned, venerable pious men, are thrust into the kennel by every ignorant labourer or dairymaid whom the devil can puff up with the monstrous self-conceit of being directly inspired from heaven? It will be a world of blood, of fury, of devastation, of each man striving for his own hand: in the end a world wrecked back into barbarism.

The judges acted strictly according to Inquisitorial law and

procedure. However, Joan, realising that she would certainly
be burnt, recanted. Within four days she revoked her recantation
and became a relapsed heretic. Now she was beyond redemption.
And the canon law fully justified the Court in sending her to the
stake.

VI

We have seen that, as Shaw says, Joan's judges were conscientious
and pious persons and the trial was a just and legal one.
But the Rouen verdict has been superseded by the verdict of history. She was rehabilitated in 1456, designated venerable in
1904, declared blessed in 1908, and finally canonised in 1920.
Therefore, two questions arise here. First, how did the Rehabilitation trial twentyfive years later reverse the verdict given at the
first trial? Secondly, how did the Church get over this verdict
when it declared Joan blessed and then canonised her five hundred
years later?

As regards the Rehabilitation, Shaw's contention is that it 'was
as corrupt as the contrary proceeding applied to Cromwell', that
it 'was really only a confirmation of the validity of the coronation
of Charles VII'. Shaw's contention, as we shall shortly see, is
right. The condemnation of Joan compromised the coronation
of Charles VII with the taint of heresy and witchcraft. Indeed,
during the trial the preacher, Erard, 'denounced her as a heretic,
and, for being assisted by her to the throne, he declared Charles
heretical also'.[71] Charles's reputation, even his legitimacy was
bound up with the reputation of Joan, and he manipulated the
Rehabilitation trial which denounced the Rouen trial as 'full of
cozenage, inconsequence, iniquity, and manifest error both in fact
and law', and declared it void on that account.

As his reputation was bound up with the reputation of Joan,
Charles VII made all attempts to ransom her, but he made these
attempts secretly, for any open attempt would have compromised
his position completely by directly implicating him in a heresy
case and alienated him from the Church of France and undermined
the cause of the Armagnac party. The University of Paris seems
to have got an inkling of such attempt. In a letter to the Duke
of Burgundy it wrote:

But we greatly fear lest through the falsity and seduction of the enemy of Hell and through the malice and subtlety of evil persons, your enemies and adversaries, who put their whole might, as it is said, to effect the deliverance of this woman by subtle means, she may in some manner be taken from your subjection (which may God prevent!).[72]

The University expressed the same fear in its letter to Jean De Luxembourg.[73] And there are some passages in the Trial Record which show that Charles had employed brother Richard and Catherine de Rochelle whom 'a white lady robed in cloth of gold' asked 'to go through the good towns with heralds, and trumpets which the King would give her, to proclaim that whosoever possessed gold, silver, or hidden treasure should immediately bring it forth; and that she would immediately know those who having any hidden did not bring it forth, and would be able easily to find it, and it should go to the paying of Joan's men-at-arms'.[74] But these efforts failed to save Joan.

Charles failed to avert Joan's condemnation but did not abandon the matter. And after working with great tenacity for twentyfive years he succeeded in bringing about the reversal of the Rouen verdict. Rightly did the English accuse him of making 'use of sinister forces', and 'the Rehabilitation was delayed by English insinuations to the Pope'.[75] Indeed, but for political exigencies, Charles would certainly not have undertaken a task that was not only arduous but risky, for the bulk of the French Church leaned to the Anglo-Burgundian party, and without strong clerical support none could hope to reverse a moral judgement that the Church iself had passed. In the Epilogue, when Ladvenu brings the news that the Rehabilitation was complete, rightly does Shaw make Charles say, 'My friend: provided they can no longer say that I was crowned by a witch and a heretic, I shall not fuss about how the trick has been done.'

From 1435 the English gradually lost ground and Charles acquired more and more power.[76] 'By 1450, Charles VII, had Rouen, the record of the Trial Proceedings, and many of those who had taken part in the trial, in his grip, so it was possible to proceed toward the rehabilitation of Joan.'[77] To pave the way for the rehabilitation, on 15 February 1450 Charles commissioned Guillaume Boville, a very influential Doctor of Theology, to

enquire into the case of Joan, with full power to summon people
and documents.[78] After examining seven witnesses Boville prepared a *Memoire* which was favourable to Joan.   Then Charles
commissioned[79] Cardinal d' Estouteville, his near relation, and
Inquisitor Brehal, 'a strong King's man', to make further enquiries
into the matter.   And he himself undertook to bear the cost of
the suits. Inquisitor Brehal 'made a series of appeals and visits
to Rome, gathered elaborate written opinions of Roman and
French ecclesiastics favourable to Joan, and submitted them
along with the proceedings of the first trial, and evidence gathered
in 1450 and 1452'.[80] And D' Estouteville 'was just the man to push
through the Rehabilitation and Charles VII by implicating him
in the proceedings, virtually forced the hand of the Pope'.[81]   To
safeguard Charles's position and camouflage political motives
the sponsors of the new move made Joan's mother appeal to remove
the stigma on the family name cast by the condemnation of Joan,
and it was Brehal who carried her appeal to Rome.   Finally on
II June 1455, Pope Calixtus III designated in a papal bull that the
case be reopened.   Thus it was the King's own interest that was
at the root of the Rehabilitation Trial.

The Rehabilitation made earnest efforts to discover legal flaws
in the trial.   Whether these flaws are real or are mere expedients
invented to undo a judgment which compromised the honour of
the King and questioned the validity of his title to the throne has
to be enquired into. It is impossible here to consider all the charges
levelled against the original trial. We shall confine ourselves to
a few that are important and relevant. These were that the Trial
Record was not authentic, because the notaries distorted it under
threats and pressure, that though declared an excommunicated
heretic, Joan was allowed to receive the Last Sacrament, that
no secular judge passed any sentence, that Cauchon had no
jurisdiction over Joan, that the judges were incompetent and partial,
that Joan's abjuration was obtained by fear and duress and that
the exhortations were full of lies and artfulness.

Manchon, Taquel, and Bois-guillaume who compiled the trial
record, were sworn notaries.[82] Bois-guillaume put his seal at the
bottom of each page and all three attested at the end. They also
bore witness to the authenticity of the Record at the Rehabilitaton,
adding 'we notaries would not have altered a word for anything
in the world, because we were not afraid of anybody'.[83]   Some

other witnesses also gave testimony to the same effect at the Rehabilitation.[84] There is little substance in the conclusion of the Rehabilitation that the notaries had falsified the Record under threats and pressure of Cauchon as deposed by some witnesses, ignoring the depositions of the notaries themselves and some others to the contrary.

The administration of the Last Sacrament to Joan is not a 'surprising anomaly' or 'an extraordinary paradox'. The last two lines of the final sentence,[85] clearly indicate that 'if true signs of penance' appeared in her 'the sacrament of penance' was to be administered to her. From the depositions of some witnesses at the Rehabilitation it is clear that on the morning of the day on which she was executed Joan had finally recanted and been admitted to penance. Jean Massieu deposed: 'On the Wednesday morning, the day on which Joan died, Friar Martin Ladvenu heard her confession,...The Bishop (asked)...Friar Martin to give her the Eucharist and anything else she might ask for.'[86] Martin Ladvenu deposed that he had 'heard Joan's confession and administered Our Lord's body to her'.[87] Thus, in view of her repentance and recantation the granting of the Last Sacrament was perfectly legal. This act reveals Cauchon's magnanimity, and not his bad conscience, as the Rehabilitation suggested.

The allegation that no secular sentence was passed before her execution is discredited by 'the letters which our Lord the King addressed to the emperor, to the kings, dukes and other princes of all Christendom'.[88] A few words from these letters will be sufficient to establish our contention : 'She was given up to the judgment of the secular power which decided that her body was to be burned',[89] she was 'abandoned to the secular justice which forthwith condemned her to be burned.'[90] These letters were written on 3 June 1431, and the allegation of the Rehabilitation twentyfive years later cannot be justified.

In the preceding section we have seen that Cauchon had jurisdiction over Joan, that he was a great jurist and canonist and that the other Judges were all eminent persons and were free from any English influence and pressure, and that they were most sincere in their admonition and exhortation and tried their utmost to save her from the fate of a heretic, as they sincerely believed her to be. The allegations of the Rehabilitation in these regards do not stand scrutiny.

The verdict of the Rehabilitation that the condemnation trial had been corrupt both in its basis and procedure is unwarranted. It was rather the Rehabilitation Trial that was vitiated by many defects and irregularities. The Rehabilitation Record is littered with hearsay evidence such as 'I have heard some people say,' 'I was told', 'It was said,' 'From what I heard', 'The current rumour was', 'It is common report', 'It was generally believed'.

Some of the judges who had condemned Joan unanimously turned their coats at the Rehabilitation only to exculpate themselves by incriminating their fellow judges who were dead.[91]   It was on the testimony of these turncoats that the Rehabilitation relied while the testimony of the upright and straightforward persons who stuck to their original conviction was ignored.   The deposition of Jean Massieu, 'a priest of doubtful morals, twice sentenced for scandalous behaviour',[92] who had performed the duties of usher in the case, was accepted as true while the deposition of Jean Beaupere, 'a famous professor' of Paris University, which delegated him as its representative at Joan's trial, was stigmatised as 'full of spleen'.   A quarter of a century had gone by and political circumstances had changed and some of the judges remembered and forgot things as political exegencies required or considerations of self interest and personal safety dictated.   One Judge, Nicolas Caval, who had been present at most of the sessions of the condemnatory trial, even denied to have been present at more than one session![93] Another judge, Andre Marguerie, deposed that 'he did not take much part in the case' although the records mention his presence at almost all the sessions![94]

Andrew Lang rightly thinks that the reticence of the Rehabilitation about the later phase of Joan's career is 'most unsatisfactory'. For Joan it was a phase of unfulfilled promise, failure, defeats, decreasing support from her followers due to their loss of faith in her divine guidance and invincibility, increasing suspicion of her heresy and witchcraft, a phase that stands in bold contrast with the earlier phase which was marked by unbroken success and victories, and implicit faith of the people in her divine mission. The Rehabilitation concentrated on Joan's earlier phase and rehabilitated her, but it was silent over her later phase which the original trial had impugned.   It seems, as Lang suggests, that the Rehabilitation tried to spare the feelings of Charles VII by drawing a veil over her later phase which was full of tormenting memories.

The Rehabilitation aimed at achieving 'a politico-religious effect' rather than making a thorough investigation.

It will be clear that the charges levelled by the Rehabilitation against the original trial are, indeed, applicable to the Rehabilitation itself. The Rehabilitation, by setting aside the Rouen verdict challenged the authority of and dealt a heavy blow at the Inquisition which was an international institution, almost infallible and impregnable. As Charles Wayland Lightbody says:

> In order to sanction the claims of Joan's conscience, and find special dispensation for her, her judges go to the antinomian extremes which would seem to leave little enough room for later Protestant agitators for the right of private judgment. Some of the views expressed by Joan's 'rehabilitators' are almost suggestive of Tolstoyan Christian philosophical anarchism.[95]

The Rehabilitation, however, despite its political motives and legal irregularities, is of the deepest importance in that it revealed the true personality of Joan, pure, divine, ineffable, who could understand the legal and theological subtleties of her judges no more than her judges could understand her divine inspiration. The Rouen Judges, as Shaw says, simply mistook a very extraordinary saint for a witch, and sent her to the stake; and posterity took five hundred years to realise that she was a saint and canonised her. And the Church canonised her without compromising its position and authority, for 'excommunication by a provincial ecclesiastical court is not one of the acts for which the Church claims infallibility'. This, I think, is an authentic story of Joan, the Maid of France, who suffered martyrdom and glorified mankind as did Jesus Christ.

Notes

[Here I have mostly referred to the authors; for the titles of the books and other details please see the bibliography on this chapter.]

1. St. John Ervine describes the occasion of the play thus:

> It was Charlotte who suggested that he should write the play, and she worked on her suggestion with great wiliness; she left books about Joan lying in every room he was likely to inhabit. He found himself

periodically picking up one of these books and reading in it, until one day he suddenly exclaimed to the wise and smiling Charlotte that he had thought of a good idea for a play. What is it, she demanded, and was told that it was about Joan of Arc. How interesting, said Charlotte! (*Bernard Shaw: His Life, Work and Friends*, p. 496).

2. Eric Bentley, *Bernard Shaw*, p. 115.

3. In the Preface to *On The Rocks* Shaw says that it was 'a drama ready made, only needing to be brought within theatrical limits and space to be a thrilling play'. p. 175.

4. *Shaw On Theatre*, edited by E.J. West, p. 278.

5. Shaw's letter to *The New York Times*, 14 September 1936 (cited in *Shaw on Theatre*, p. 245).

6. *Bernard Shaw*, pp. 157–8.

7. The statement of Maurice Colbourne (*The Real Bernard Shaw*, p. 199) that Shaw wrote the play 'with no inspiration from the usual Shavian fires...no devotion to Creative Evolution, or other theory...', cannot be justified.

8. *The Art of Bernard Shaw*, p. 105.

9. A.C. Ward, *Bernard Shaw*, p. 159.

10. St. John Ervine, *Bernard Shaw : His Life, Work and Friends*, p. 72.

11. *English Drama: A Modern Viewpoint* op. cit., p. 117.

12. *British Drama*, op. cit., p. 286.

13. Archibald Henderson: *Bernard Shaw: Playboy and Prophet*, p. 543.

14. *Shaw*, p. 163.

15. *A Critical History of English Literature*, pp. 1106–7.

16. *The Art of Bernard Shaw*, p. 103.

17. *A Guide to the Plays of Bernard Shaw*, p. 280.

18. *Inquisition and Liberty*, p. 335.

19. Ibid., p. 355.

20. *Bernard Shaw: Playboy and Prophet* op. cit., p. 542.

21. *Shaw: His Life, Work and Friends*, p. 500.

22. *Shaw*, p. 163.

23. p. 170.

24. *Bernard Shaw*, p. 116

25. Desmond MacCarthy, *Shaw*, p. 167.

26. *Bernard Shaw: Playboy and Prophet* op. cit., p. 546.

27. *Narrative and Dramatic Sources of Shakespeare*, vol. III, p. 25.

28. *The Life of Joan of Arc*, vol. I, p. XXI.

29. Charles Wayland Lightbody, op. cit., p. 30.

30. G.G. Coulton, op. cit., p. 118.

31. W.P. Barrett, p. 2.

32. Ibid., pp. 21–134.

33. Ibid., pp. 140–224.

34. Ibid., pp. 264–7.

35. Ibid., pp. 167–79.

36. Ibid., pp. 279–80.

37. Ibid., pp. 280–2.

38. Ibid., pp. 282–300.

39. Ibid., pp. 306–11.
40. Ibid., pp. 312–43.
    W.S. Scott, *Joan*, pp. 163–4.
    V. Sackville-West, *Saint Joan*, pp. 353–4.
    Anatole France, *Life of Joan*, vol III, pp. 159–64.
    Mark Twain, *Personal Recollections of Joan*, vol II, p. 251.
    R. Gower, *Joan of Arc*, pp. 232–3.
    Milton Waldman, *Joan*, pp. 306–8.
    T.D. Murray, *Jeanne*, pp. 130–2.
41. W.P. Barrett, *The Trial*, pp. ?14–16.
    W.S. Scott, *Life*, p. 165.
    V. Sackville-West, *St. Joan*, p. 358.
    Anatole France, *Life of Joan* vol. III, p. 164.
    T.D. Murray, *Jeanne*, pp. 132–3.
42. W.P. Barrett, pp. 319–20; V. Sackville-West, pp. 363-4.
43. W.P. Barrett, pp. 19–20, 22–3.
44. Charles Wayland Lightbody, p. 104.
45. W.P. Barrett, pp. 22–31.
46. Ibid., pp. 287–95.
47. Ibid., p. 2.
48. Ibid., p. 33–5.
49. Ibid., pp. 285–7.
50. Ibid., p. 132.
51. Ibid., pp. 279–80; Waldman, p. 298.
52. Regine Pernoud, pp. 180-1, 194; V. Sackville-West, p. 355; Milton Waldman, p. 307.
53. W.P. Barrett, p. 14 (see also Regine Pernoud, p. 48; Anatole France, vol. III, p. 163; T.D. Murray, p. 187).
54. p. 107.
55. W.P. Barrett, p. 240.
56. p. 256.
57. Preface, p. 28.
58. W.P. Barrett, p. 277.
59. Ibid., p. 278.
60. Ibid., p. 278.
61. Ibid., p. 70; T.D. Murray, p. 137.
62. W.P. Barrett, pp. 51–2 (see also L.R. Gower, pp. 156–7; Milton Waldman, pp. 253–4; T.D. Murray, p. 7; A.B. Paine, p. 206).
63. Ibid., p. 50 (see also Mark Twain, vol, II, p. 128; Gower, p. 154; Milton Waldman, p. 250; T.D. Murray, p. 5; A.B. Paine, p. 205).
64. Ibid., p. 54.
65. Ibid., p. 59.
66. Ibid., p. 63 (see also L.R. Gower, p. 170; George Bernanos, p. 9; Milton Waldman, p. 262; T.D. Murray, p. 18).
67. Ibid., pp. 67, 75, 83, 85, 93; T.D. Murray, pp. 9, 15, 17, 18, 45, 69, 80.
68. W.P. Barrett, pp. 53–4.
69. *Inquisition and Liberty*, pp. 58, 59. (Milton Waldman says: 'If Cauchon

had chosen he could have stopped the proceedings then and there and ordered the executioner to make ready the stake.' p. 253).

70. W.P. Barrett, pp. 306–9 (see also George Bernanos, pp. 42–7; Milton Waldman, pp. 302–3; T.D. Murray, pp. 122–6).
71. Ibid., p. 8; Regine Pernoud, pp. 9, 13, 26.
72. W.P. Barrett, p. 23.
73. Ibid., p. 24; Waldman, p. 225.
74. W.P. Barrett, pp. 89–90, 205–6.
75. Charles Wayland Lightbody, p. 116.
76. See John Richard Green, *A Short History of the English People*, pp. 280–1; Regine Pernoud, pp. 1–17.
77. Charles Wayland Lightbody, p. 121.
78. Regine Pernoud, p. 1.
79. Ibid., pp. 10–13.
80. Charles Wayland Lightbody, pp. 122–3.
81. Ibid., p. 123.
82. W.P. Barrett, p. 40.
83. Regine Pernoud, pp. 38–45.
84. Ibid., p. 195; T. Douglas Murray, p. 187 (evidence of Brother Pierre Migier).
85. W.P. Barrett, p. 331.
86. Regine Pernoud, p. 185; T.D. Douglas, p. 176.
87. Regine Pernoud p. 187 (see also V. Sackville-West, p. 336; Anatole France, vol. III, p. 176; T.D. Murray, pp. 193, 206–7).
88. W.P. Barrett, pp. 339–46.
89. Ibid., p. 342.
90. Ibid., p. 346.
91. There was no general indictment of the judges who had condemned Joan to the stake. Only a few of them were selected to be scapegoats for the assumed miscarriage of justice, and 'those all safely dead and beyond the reach of judical recriminations' (Charles Wayland Lightbody, p. 136). Cauchon, the Bishop of Beauvais, and D' Estivet, the Promoter, were dead, and the Vice Inquisitor John Lemaitre could not be found. (Regine Pernoud, pp. 36–37, 47; Anatole France, vol. III, pp. 219, 222).
92. Regine Pernoud, p. 12.
93. Ibid., p. 195.
94. Ibid., pp. 192–3.
95. *The Judgments of Joan*, p. 128.

5. In Good King Charles's Golden Days

In Good King Charles's Golden Days is a scintillating comedy, written when Shaw was eightythree years old. The play reveals Shaw's amazing vitality, his mental alertness, his versatility, his wit, his irrepressible comic sense, his grasp of character and his delicate sense of style. A combination of such excellences is rarely found in an octogenarian. All his life Shaw challenged current thought and doctrine in every direction, contradicted everybody and everything and wrote with the deliberate object of forcing the public to reconsider its morals; there is not a subject which did not come within the ambit of his caustic pen—science, literature, art, politics, economics, health, racial prejudices, social standards, medicine, religion. He had his pet doctrines, and he advocated them dogmatically. But *In Good King Charles's Golden Days* we have a different picture of Shaw. He has laid aside his dogmatism, he has laid aside his pugnacity. And he appears as an old philosopher preaching no positive doctrine, pronouncing no verdict, working out no philosophical system, but pleasantly talking on a number of subjects he had so repeatedly talked on before—religion, art, science, kingcraft; and a number of *obiter dicta* about life, about the still small voice of conscience, of beauty and design, about the function of wives and mistresses add grace and charm to the discussion. Shaw postulates questions and states problems through the mouths of persons who are conscious of their implications, but he does not give any final answers, nor does he make any attempt to solve the problems.

Here Shaw is preoccupied with ideas, but the ideas spring from no general philosophy. The play has no plot, and the characters, generally express opinions on various problems from a Shavian point of view. Shaw talks through them on a variety of subjects as his fancy dictates; the play is an endless talk, and the talk is often talk for talk's sake. Yet the play has characteristics that make it an admirable work of art.

In spite of his preoccupation with ideas, Shaw possesses the qualities demanded of a great playwright. *In Good King Charles's Golden Days* is more like a Platonic Symposium than a play. It sparkles from first to last with rich, sagacious and witty conversation on a variety of subjects.   But Shaw also makes use of effects which are theatrically striking.   The play is divided into two acts —the first act is very long, running to sixtytwo pages, and the second act, which is very short, is like an epilogue to the first. In the first act Shaw assembles in Isaac Newton's house at Cambridge in the year 1680 Charles II, George Fox, Newton and Kneller; also Charles' mistresses Nell Gwynn, Barbara Villiers. Louise De Keroualle, Newton's housekeeper Mrs. Basham and his maidservant Sally, and Charles' brother James.   The four protagonists—Charles II, George Fox, Newton and Kneller— are leaders in their own spheres of kingship, religion, science and art.   They express their views on their respective subjects through a conversation that seems never to come to an end.   The unending dialogue is highly intellectual, and it is difficult to maintain mental alertness at so long a stretch.   In lesser hands the long discussion would have flagged.   But Shaw has adopted certain devices to make it extremely lively, exhilarating and captivating.   The diversity of the subjects discussed and the *obiter dicta* scattered throughout the play keep the audience alert and curious.   The clash among the protagonists—the intellectual tussle is the theme of the drama.   The jealousies and tantrums of the mistresses of Charles II, the clash between the protagonists and the women, and the repeated intrusion of Mrs. Basham upon the intellectual talk of the protagonists are all meant to relieve the intellectual tension. And the 'knock-about' between Isaac Newton and the Duke of York is introduced to give relief to the audience.   The second act which shows a shift in place without disturbing the unity of time, takes us to the boudoir of Queen Catherine of Braganza in Newmarket.   The hearty conversation between Charles II and his queen Catherine is intended to reveal the deeper basis of the relation between the two.   Charles has many mistresses, but they can in no way interfere with his permanent marriage relationship; the husband is never really unfaithful to his wife, and the wife is ever devoted to her husband. The conversation is written with gusto and is immensely enjoyable.   The *obiter dicta* about conscience, about love, about how to choose rulers and so on act as diversion.   And the rhythm and the emotional content of a few passages help to keep the audience spell-bound.   One such passage is Newton's reply to Kneller's contemptuous statement that to the scientist 'the universe is merely but a clock' that begins with 'Shall I tell you a secret, Mr. Beautymonger?' George Fox's speech beginning with 'All, all, all of them. They are snares of the devil' and Kneller's speech beginning with 'And whose hand is it if not the hand of God!' are two more passages of such captivating poetic appeal.

In Good King Charles's Golden Days is a *tour de force*. And rightly did *The Times* comment on 12 August 1939 that 'most of our best authors of comedy today sit at Mr. Shaw's feet.... What is the explanation? It is surely that Mr. Shaw is a model dramatist in spite of his preoccupation with so-called ideas, not because of them, and that the secret of his dramatist's impulse is in his irrepressible comic sense.'

It will be evident from our discussion that the charge so often levelled against Shaw that he is not a dramatist, that he uses the stage only as a platform from which to preach his sermons is erroneous and baseless. Another charge that must be rejected is that Shaw's characters are puppets created to express his own opinions and personal emotions and impulses, not creatures of flesh and blood. In this play most of the characters are historical figures but they are as human and interesting as our contemporaries. They are all well defined and 'stamped with the ineradicable lines of life'. And although sometimes they express their creator's views, they are full of idiosyncrasies of their own. C.E.M. Joad's statement that 'the characters are less human beings than abstractions, consisting only of so much of a man as is necessary to fill the role of mouthpiece for a particular point of view',[1] is misconceived.

II

Shaw is not interested in writing a historical romance with Charles II as the hero and one of his mistresses as the heroine. Nor does he find any novelty in writing a chronicle play about Charles II, for the political facts of Charles's reign have often been recorded by modern historians of all parties, from the Whig Macaulay to the Jacobite Hilaire Belloc.

But when we turn from the sordid facts of Charles's reign, and from his Solomonic polygamy, to what might have happened to him but did not, the situation becomes interesting and fresh. For instance, Charles might have met that human prodigy Isaac Newton. And Newton might have met that prodigy of another sort, George Fox, the founder of the morally mighty Society of Friends, vulgarly called the Quakers. Better again, all three might have met.[2]

In this play Shaw assembles in the house of Newton four notable personages of Charles's reign—Charles II, Newton, Kneller, and Fox, who in reality never met anywhere. The incidents in the play never occurred, and, Shaw says, 'yet any one reading this play or witnessing a performance of it will not only be pleasantly amused, but will come out with a knowledge of the dynamics of Charles's reign; that is, of the political and personal forces at work in it, that ten years of digging up mere facts in the British Museum or the Record Office could not give.'[3] In the preface Shaw claims that in this play he has rendered 'an act of historical justice' to Charles II whose notoriety as a wenching trifler has obscured his political ability and eclipsed the fact that he was the best of husbands. And we have to examine how far Shaw has been faithful to history in his portraiture of Charles II.

In this play Charles II makes his first appearance, under the *nom de plume* of Mr. Rowley, accompanied by twelve spaniels which he is very fond of. It is 1680 and the king is fifty; he is very tall and captivating, too lazy and addicted beyond measure to sensual indulgence but very hard working on occasions, keenly interested in science, an interminable talker, constantly in money difficulties. Broadly speaking, in all this Shaw follows history faithfully. Take, for example, his impecuniosity. Richard Lodge says, 'Not only did Charles never recover from the financial troubles of his exile and the first year of his reign, he was never able to defray his expenses from his normal revenue. Chronic impecuniosity, always verging upon bankruptcy, and on one occasion actually crossing the borderline, gives the clue to many of the problems of the reign.'[4] As regards his interest in science, 'Charles was interested in science, had his own laboratory and gave the Royal Society its charter. He encouraged applied science.'[5] Charles's laziness and excessive addiction to sexual pleasure, his impecuniosity, his interest in science, his fondness for spaniels are amply testified to by all historians—Macaulay, John Richard Green, G.N. Clark, Richard Lodge, Trevelyan.

Shaw's Charles II, like his Julius Caesar, is a realist. After a prolonged exile he ascends the throne at a time when England is seething with the turmoil of political, religious and personal quarrels. The enemies of monarchy had beheaded his father, and although monarchy has been set up again it is not secure. As he tells George Fox, he had 'had enough of the gutter', and he is now determined not 'to go on his travels again', as Nell says. In these critical times it is his realistic attitude towards life and the world that enables him, as he says, 'to keep my crown on my head and my head on my shoulders' and guide the state through its many crises. His practical shrewdness is clearly revealed in his analysis of the current political situation. He is fully conscious of the fact that since his 'father's business is abolished in England', he is 'far less important now in England than Jack the fish hawker.' His brother James, a 'Popish Blockhead', says, 'When I am King—as I shall be, in my own right, and not by the leave of any parliamentary gang—I shall restore the Church and restore the monarchy: Yes, the monarchy, Charles; for there has been no real restoration.' James has neither foresight nor hindsight and thinks he will be able to impose his will upon the people and reign by divine right, and 'Europe will see them crumble up like moths in a candle flame.' But Charles is realistic enough to realise that monarchy is gone and that its sanctions and foundations are now political rather than divine or traditional and that he has to keep the crown by his wits. He hates 'blood and battles' and nothing frightens him so much as James's 'stupid pluck'. And with an almost prophetic insight into the future he tells James, 'They will have your head off inside of five years unless you jump into the nearest fishing smack and land in France.' And he thinks it would be far kinder of him 'to push the Exclusion Bill through and save you from the fate of our father'.

As a realist Charles looks at everything from the point of view of expediency. In all critical situations he acts with duplicity and manoeuvres and manipulates people and events to his own advantage. It is because of this capacity for manipulation that he can justifiably say that 'I am the King of England; and my head is still on my shoulders.' Self-interest being his only motive, he has discarded all religious scruples. In his attitude towards the

Church his feelings are political rather than religious. His sympathies are on the side of Catholicism because the Catholics form a large part of the population enjoying great political importance, but he has 'to manage Protestants who are so frightfully cruel that I dare not interfere with Protestant judges who are merciless'. He says, 'There are only two horses in the race now: the Protestant and the Catholic. I have to ride both at once.' Titus Oates, the fabricator of the Popish Plot, must be lodged at his palace at Whitehall with a pension of four hundred pounds a year, for he is the most popular man in England at present. He tells James, 'The Protestants will have you, Jamie, by hook or crook: I foresee that: they are the real men of blood. But they shall not have me. I shall die in my bed, and die King of England inspite of them.' And George Fox aptly observes, 'This is not kingcraft : it is chicanery.' He shows the same dexterity in the double game he plays with the Whigs and the Tories. He tells George Fox, 'Even I, the head of the Church, the Defender of the Faith, stand between the Whigs who suspect me of being a Papist and the Tories who suspect me of being an atheist.' The words of Barbara clearly sum up Charles's religious attitude: 'He has always defied God and betrayed women. He does not know the meaning of the word religion. He laughed at it in France. He hated it in Scotland. In England he believes nothing.'

Always guided by motives of self-interest, Charles is not only a man of no faith but also a man of no principles. James rightly says, '...you have no faith, no principles: you do not believe in anything.' He is prepared to submit to much which he deems humiliating rather than go on his travels again. He believes in the prerogatives of the Crown and is opposed to Parliament which is 'the very diwle' and yet he allows it to interfere and to assert its rights, for to attempt to have his own way against a powerful parliament would be to risk his kingship. He believes in the Stuart theory of the Divine Right of kings but laughs it down the wind, because 'with the Protestants you do not succeed by divine right'. He tells Catherine:

How often have I told you that I am no real King: that the utmost I can do is to keep my crown on my head and my head on my shoulders. How often have you asked me to do some big thing like joining your Church, or some little thing like pardoning a priest or a quaker condemned to some cruel punishment! And you have found that outside the court, where my smiles and my frowns count for everything, I have no power. The perjured scoundrel, Titus Oates, steeped in unmentionable vices, is lodged in my palace with a pension. If I could have my way he would be lodged on the gallows. There is a preacher named Bunyan who has written a book about the Christian life that is being read, they tell me, all the world over; and I could not release him from Bedford Gaol, where he rotted for years.

We may pause here to examine whether Shaw's picture of Charles II as a realist without any religious or moral principles, looking at everything from the point of view of expediency and thus achieving political success is in accord with history. Richard Lodge speaks of his 'duplicity which was gradually becoming a settled nature to him'.[6] To avoid being forced down from the throne he used his political power and stooped to all sorts of dissimulation. As Trevelyan says, 'half his art was to prevent his adversaries from discovering till too late that he had any political ability at all'.[7] That he was always guided by motives of self interest is amply testified to by John Richard Green : 'Gratitude he had none, for he looked upon self interest as the only motive of men's actions....'[8] That he believed in the prerogatives of the king and was opposed to parliament and yet for personal security and personal gains allowed it to interfere and assert rights will be evident from the following passage:

But he believed as firmly as his father or his grandfather had believed in the other prerogatives of the Crown; and like them, he looked on Parliaments, with suspicion and jealousy. 'He told Lord Essex', Burnet says, 'that he did not wish to be like a grand Signior, with some mutes about him, and bags of bowstrings to strangle men; but he did not think he was a king so long as a company of fellows were looking into his actions, and examining his ministers as well as his accounts.' 'A King', he thought, 'who might be checked, and have his ministers called to an account, was but a king in name.' In other words, he had no settled plan of tyranny, but he meant to rule as independently as he could, and from the beginning to the end of his reign there never

was a moment when he was not doing something to carry out
his aim.   But he carried it out in a tentative, irregular fashion
which it was as hard to detect as to meet.   Whenever there
was any strong opposition, he gave way.   If popular feeling
demanded the dismissal of his ministers, he dismissed them.   If
it protested against his declaration of indulgence, he recalled it.
If it cried for victims in the frenzy of the Popish Plot, he gave it
victims till the frenzy was at an end.   It was easy for Charles to
yield and to wait, and just as easy for him to take up the thread
of his purpose again the moment the pressure was over.[9]

That in religious matters his feelings were political rather than religious is clearly stated by Trevelyan: 'Charles politically abandoned
Catholicism, but not absolutism. He would have preferred
to found a Catholic monarchy on the French model; he was per-
force content to reign as a professing Protestant.'[10]   Charles's
political capacity that enabled him to keep 'my crown on my head
and my head on my shoulders' is testified to by Trevelyan who
looks upon him as 'one of the greatest politicians who ever
succeeded in the struggle for power in England'.

Shaw represents Charles as using Louise de Keroualle as an
agent for extracting money from the king of France giving 'little
enough' in return.   Here Shaw has taken outrageous liberty with
history.   The truth is that Louise de Keroualle was sent by Louis
XIV to act as his spy on Charles II.   She became the most influential woman in the English Court and succeeded in winning
Charles to French interests.   And 'Louis XIV recognised his
obligations by conferring upon her the valuable fief of Aubigny.
She represents the continuance of the policy of the treaty of Dover
and the enslavement of England to France.'[11]   Here Shaw's
departure from history seems to be deliberate, his purpose being
to emphasise Charles's policy of expediency which finds French
money as good as English money if 'little enough' is to be given
in return for it.   But there is not a scrap of evidence to support
Shaw's assertion in the Preface that Charles 'made use of Louise:
there is no evidence that she made use of him. To the Whig historians the transaction makes Charles a quisling in the service
of Louis and a traitor to his country. This is mere protestant
scurrility: the only shady part of it is that Charles, spending the
money in the service of England, gave *Le Roi Soleil* no value for it.'

III

Let us now turn to Shaw's picture of Charles II in respect of his sexual relations and see how far it is true to history. Charles is in the library of Newton's house in Cambridge conversing with the scientist and George Fox. Three of his mistresses—Nell Gwynn, Barbara Villiers and Louise de Keroualle—appear there separately. Nelly complains that she has been kept waiting in the street too long, but is never ruffled. Barbara bursts into the room 'in a tearing rage', storms and rants and accuses Charles of being unfaithful to her a thousand times and suggests that he should kill her and 'be happy with that low stage player'. The designing Louise is the last to come.

Historians are unanimous in their opinion that Charles's sexual conduct, like that of his equally sagacious grandfather, was scandalous and that he had too many mistresses, Barbara, Nell Gwynn and Louise De Keroualle being only three of them. The skill with which Shaw seizes on the essential characteristics of each of these three mistresses is admirable. Shaw's Barbara is not only famous for her tantrums but, as Charles tells Catherine, is 'a woman who thought of nothing but her body and its satisfaction, which meant men and money. For both, Barbara is insatiable. Grab, grab, grab.' That she was so is testified to by Richard Lodge who says that even the Chancellor and the Treasurer could not 'check the rapacity of Barbara Palmer', that 'Charles was already wearied of the shrewish scoldings and shameless misconduct of Lady Castlemaine'.

Shaw has portrayed Nell Gwynn as a famous actress who has 'the gutter in [her] blood'; she is unsophisticated, compliant and adorable and is a source of comfort and peace to Charles who likes her most because 'nothing can make a courtier of her'. Charles tells Barbara: 'You are like a dairymaid: you think there is no end to a King's money. Here is my Nelly, who is more careful of my money than she is of her own. Well, when I am dying, and all the rest of you are forgotten, my last thought will be of Nelly.' Shaw's picture of Nell Gwynn is authentic. 'Nell Gwynn, an actress, was the most popular of the mistresses, and Charles appreciated her wit.'[12]

Louise de Keroualle, who at 30 retains her famous babyish beauty and whom the English called Madame Carwell, is presented

as a typical Frenchwoman possessing all the temperamental
peculiarities of her race and sex. She comes to Newton, the
alchemist, to have a love charm which would make Charles love
her only and not everybody, because 'he is far too amorous of
every pretty woman he meets'. She succeeds in getting a prescription from Newton and his word of honour that he would give this
prescription to no other woman of the court. She must have
influence over the king but her ascendency is often threatened by
the other mistresses, and hence she must have some love charm.
That Shaw's portrait of Louise de Keroualle is authentic will be
evident from the following passage from Richard Lodge:

> The very contrast may have helped to attract him [Charles] to the
> childish, simple and baby face of Louise de Keroualle, a young
> Breton lady....Madame Carwell, as the English called her,
> was on account of her foreign origin by far the most unpopular
> of the king's mistresses. Charles was no more constant to her
> than he had been to Lady Castlemaine and from time to time her
> ascendency was seriously threatened. But her influence was
> never completely overthrown, and she continued to be the
> most influential woman at the English court until Charles's
> death.[13]

But, as has already been shown, Shaw has taken liberty with history
in making Louise de Keroualle Charles's agent for sponging on
King Louis XIV.

It may be pointed out in passing that by making the three
mistresses pursue Charles to the house of Newton Shaw illustrates
his theory that woman is the hunter and man the game, a theory
that he had already elaborated in many of his earlier dramas,
especially in *Man and Superman*. Louise de Keroualle, of course,
denies having pursued Charles. 'I came to consult Mr. Newton,
the alchemist', she says. Her purpose, as she tells Newton priva-
tely, is to get a love charm to captivate the King, which too
illustrates Shaw's thesis. Later she also admits that when she
was sent to England to captivate Charles she herself was captivated
by Charles's 'seventy inches and [his] good looks'.

Incidentally it may be pointed out here that the encounter of
Newton with the three mistresses of Charles is meant to illustrate
Shaw's thesis that the real conflict of life is between genius and

sexual attraction. When Nelly proposes to come to him again Newton says, 'No no no no no, Madam, I cannot entertain ladies. They do not fit into my way of life.' As Shaw says in *Man And Superman* in the Epistle Dedicatory To Arthur Bingham Walkey, 'When it comes to sex relations, the man of genius does not share the common man's danger of capture.'

Shaw's Charles at the age of fifty has learnt too much about women and love, and thinks that 'the women themselves are worse penances than any priest dare inflict on you'. He has learnt that 'bodies are all alike: all cats are grey in the dark. It is the souls and the brains that are different.' And he now loves his wife Catherine truly and realises her superiority over her mistresses. He has finished with all women and says, 'There is nobody like a wife.' Charles's relations with Catherine are shown to be a model of tenderness, appreciation and reverence. Charles thinks that to be Catherine's husband is 'a great privilege'. And Catherine looks upon Charles as 'the very best of husbands that ever lived'. Charles now repents that he treated her very badly when he was a young man and tells her, 'We must forget our foolish youth : we are grown up now.' He would now do anything to make up for his unfaithfulness. He asks, 'Beloved: can anything I can ever do make up to you for my unfaithfulness?' But his wife does not mind his sex adventures, for she knows that he can never be unfaithful to her: 'People think of nothing but that, as if that were the whole life. What care I about your women? Your concubines? Your handmaidens? The servants of your common pleasures? They have set me free to be something more to you than they are or can ever be. You have never been really unfaithful to me.' Shaw's contention is that many historians and many dramatists, by representing Charles as an unfaithful husband, have given a misleading picture of the king. His picture only, he claims, is correct.

Every historian mentions Charles's profligacy and his neglect and ill treatment of his wife. Trevelyan, for example, says, 'Catherine of Braganza, an unfortunate woman from a Portuguese cloister, was brought over, married and held upto ridicule by her husband, who compelled her, in spite of tears and fainting fits to employ the Castlemaine as her own lady of the bedchamber.'[14] Richard Lodge speaks of the 'cynical brutality' with which Charles overcame the young queen's repugnance to admit Lady

Castlemaine to be a lady of her bedchamber. Catherine of
Braganza, however, gradually resigned herself to fate and ceased
to be sensitive with regard to her husband's infidelity. And
Charles did not subject to further ill treatment the innocent woman
whom he had so grossly injured. Shaw has represented her
resignation to fate as her superior attitude to sexual infidelity
and Charles's compassion for much injured wife as genuine love
and devotion. And in the Preface he argues, like a defending
attorney, with persuasiveness and incomparable oratory and, like
a judge, declares to have given a correct picture and 'rendered the
Merry Monarch an act of historical justice'. But, as will be evident
from our discussion, this picture has no relation to reality, and his
assertion that Charles was the best of husbands who 'took his
marriage very seriously and his sex adventures as calls of nature
on an entirely different footing' is pure Shavianism according to which
sex is a mere instrument of creation which does not discriminate
between marital relations and extra marital sex adventures.

IV

Shaw often uses men and women to voice his own opinions. *In
Good King Charles's Golden Days* is not a didactic play—a play
with a purpose, and yet, as is Shaw's wont, on several occasions
he makes Charles express some views he himself had repeatedly
preached all his life. Shaw had bitter experiences at schools, which
he describes as 'damnable boy prisons' and his years there were a
sheer waste of time. These boyhood experiences coloured his
attitude towards education. In *Sixteen Self Sketches* he says
that at his schools he 'was clearly learning nothing except that
[he] had better not have learnt', and he calls the schoolmaster an
'executioner', 'the vilest abortionist', 'the enemy of mankind'.
In the Preface to *Misalliance* he says, 'My schooling did me a
great deal of harm and no good whatever', and he concludes that
'the education is sham. Those who have been taught most know
least.' Charles II never paid any serious thought to the question
of education, nor did he ever pass any judgement on the contemporary system of education. Shaw's Charles is opposed to the
kind of education prevailing in schools. He holds that schools
are worse than useless and one has to unlearn what one learns
there. George Fox says, 'I am not schooled and learned as you

two princes are.' To this Charles says, 'Thank your stars for that, Pastor: You have nothing to unlearn.' Again, Charles tells Catherine that 'learning Latin is no use: Jack Churchill, who is an ignoramus, is worth fifty scholars'. Here, if anywhere, we hear the voice of Shaw himself, inveighing against the prevailing system of education.

As I have pointed out in my *George Bernard Shaw's Philosophy of Life*, for more than two decades before his death Shaw was preoccupied with two problems: first, the economic problem of how to distribute the wealth of the world and second, the political problem of how to choose rulers and prevent them from abusing their authority. He believes that Nature always produces more than the necessary percentage of persons gifted with sufficient political sagacity to rule and this belief finds expression in the prefaces of several plays as well as in his prose works. *In Everybody's Political What's What*, for example, he says, 'Nature miraculously provides the necessary number of persons thus specially gifted and always provides them in excess.' But the question that engaged Shaw's attention was how to decide upon who are fit to choose the specially gifted rulers. And he advocates the elimination of natural ignorance by making a compulsory up-to-date education within everyone's reach. Shaw is Platonic in his preoccupation with the question of how to choose rulers and in his emphasis on the importance and need of education for this purpose. In this play Charles tells Catherine, 'No beloved: the problem of how to choose a ruler is still unanswered; and it is the riddle of civilization.' Charles does not attempt to solve the problem but shrewdly hints the direction in which an answer can be found when he says: 'I tell you again there are in England, or in any other country, the makings of half a dozen kings and councils; but they are mostly in prison. If we only knew how to pick them out and label them, then the people would have their choice out of the half dozen. It may end that way, but not before they are chosen.' Certainly Charles, who was all for constitutional monarchy, would never have talked like this. Unmistakably in this passage Shaw has made him spout his own ideas as to how to choose rulers.

Shaw holds a firm opinion about most of the races and nationalties of the world in general. The English he looks upon as a non-adult race, without brains. The Scots, on the other hand,

are very intelligent and far superior to the English. Shaw's
arraignment of the English and his praise of the Scots are found
in many of his plays. Napoleon, in *The Man of Destiny*, tells
the Strange Lady that the English, 'a nation of shopkeepers', are
'a race apart'. He diagnoses her to be English on the basis of the
tricks she plays on him to get the letters but grants that her 'brains
are not English'. Later he discovers that her grandmother was Irish,
a fact that accounts for her brains. In 'The Thing Happens' (*Back
to Mathuselah*), Archbishop Haslam tells Burge-Lubin that the
English 'are a non-adult race; and the Irish and the Scots, and the
niggers and Chinks, as you call them, though their lifetime is as
short as ours, or shorter, yet do somehow contrive to grow up a
little before they die'. In *The Apple Cart*, Proteus exclaims, 'God
help England if she had no Scots to think for her.' Charles II, in
In Good King Charles's Golden Days, tells Catherine that brains 'are
no use here: the English will not be ruled; and there is nothing
they hate like brains. For brains and religion you must go to
Scotland;..., Again he tells her, 'No: give me English birds and
English trees, English dogs and Irish horses, English rivers and
English ships; but Englishmen! No, No. No.' These speeches are
clear echoes of Shaw's opinion about the English scattered through
his writings.

There is a passage of dialogue between Charles and Catherine
which, as St. John Ervine says, reveals 'the essential wisdom
of G.B.S'.[15] The passage deserves to be cited here.

CATHERINE: Our consciences, which come from God, must be
all the same.
CHARLES: They are not. Do you think God so stupid that he
could invent only one sort of conscience?
CATHERINE: (*Shocked*): What a dreadful thing to say! I must not
listen to you.
CHARLES: No two consciences are the same. No two love
affairs are the same. No two marriages are the same. No two
illnesses are the same. No two children are the same. No two
human beings are the same. What is right for one is wrong for
the other. Yet they cannot live together without laws; and a
law is something that obliges them all to do the same thing.

V

As regards Newton, Shaw boastfully says, 'Not since Shakespeare made Hector of Troy quote Aristotle has the stage perpetrated a more staggering anachronism.' Shaw has taken outrageous liberties with the facts of Newton's life. The first act of the play is set in a house of Newton in the town of Cambridge, but Newton never had such a house in Cambridge. Shaw represents Newton as 'the greatest man alive' in the year 1680, but the truth is that in 1680 he was unknown outside a small circle of scientific friends. As T.B. Macaulay says, even 'in the year 1685 his fame, though splendid was only dawning',[16] his *Principia*, which made him widely popular, being published in 1687. Shaw's Newton says that he has discovered 'a force in nature which I call gravitation'. But the idea of universal gravitation did not find any expression till the publication of the *Principia* in 1687. In this play Newton refers to his chronological history of the world to the writing of which he has devoted months of his life. But, as Brewster says, this chronological history was completed 'at the time of his death, and it was published in 1728'.[17] Newton's awareness of something 'amiss with the perihilion of mercury', his horror at Einsteinian curvature, Godfrey Kneller's idea that 'the line of beauty is a curve', which was Hogarth's idea expressed about half a century after the supposed date of this play (1680) are three more anachronisms in the play. Such instances of anachronism are plentifully found here. Lord Keynes aptly says, 'G.B.S. allows the characters of his play to be acquainted with works of Newton which were not published until decades later.'[18]

Shaw's Newton, aged thirtyeight, is proud, vain and ill-tempered. His encounter with Kneller, George Fox and James reveals this aspect of his character. He thinks he 'was born one of the greatest mathematicians of the world'. He tells Charles that he has 'devoted months of [his] life to the writing of a book—a chronology of the world—which would have cost any man other than Isaac Newton twenty years hard labour'. He calls George Fox an infidel and asks him to leave his house. He calls James a 'Popish blockhead', rises in a fury and tells him menacingly: 'Will you leave my house, or shall I throw you out through the window?' Kneller says that Newton is 'a most over-weening, a most audacious man'. No doubt Newton was conscious of his greatness and

knew his place as a 'philosopher',[19] but pride in his knowledge,
vanity, arrogance and irritability have been falsely attributed to
him by Shaw. David Brewster says, 'The social character of
Sir Isaac Newton was such as might have been expected from his
intellectual attainments. He was modest, candid, and affable,
and without any of the eccentricities of genius, suiting himself to
every company, and speaking of himself and others in such a manner
that he was never even suspected of vanity.'[20] From his daily
experience Dr. Pemberton says that neither Newton's 'extreme
great age, nor his universal reputation had rendered him stiff in
opinion, or in any degree elated'.[21] Newton was extremely
modest, and his modesty arose out of a consciousness of what a
small portion of nature he had been able to examine and how much
remained to be explored. Shaw's Newton justly says, 'I spend
my life contemplating the ocean of my ignorance. I once boasted
of having picked up a pebble on the endless beach of that ocean.
I should have said a grain of sand.' Newton uttered this sentiment
not in 1680 but a short time before his death in 1727. Shaw has
also altered the words of this memorable sentiment which has
been recorded thus: 'I do not know what I may appear to the
world; but to myself I seem to have been only like a boy playing
on the sea shore, and diverting myself in now and then finding a
smoother pebble or a prettier shell than ordinary, whilst the great
ocean of truth lay all undiscovered before me.'[22]

Shaw's play abounds in anachronisms, contradictions and
distortions of this kind. However, Shaw has given an account of
certain things about Newton quite authentically. Shaw's Newton
believes in the transmutation of base metals into gold, the Elixir
of life and the philosopher's stone. He says:

There are so many more interesting things to be worked at:
the transmutations of matter, the elixir of life, the magic of
light and color, above all, the secret meaning of the Scriptures.
And when I should be concentrating my mind on these I find
myself wandering off into idle games of speculation about
numbers in infinite series, and dividing curves into indivisibly
short triangle bases. How silly! What a waste of time, priceless
time!

David Brewster says that Newton 'had been a diligent student of

Jacob Behmen's writings and that there were found among his papers copious abstracts from them in his own handwriting.... Sir Isaac, together with one Dr. Newton, his relation, had, in the earlier part of his life, set up furnaces, and were for several months at work in quest of the philosopher's tincture.'[23] Lord Keynes says,

As many hundreds of unpublished manuscript survive to testify, Newton was seeking the philosopher's stone, the Elixir of life and the transmutation of base metals into gold. He was, indeed, a magician who believed that by intense concentration of mind on traditional hermetics and revealed books he could discover the secrets of nature and the course of future events, just as by the pure play of mind on a few facts of observation he had unveiled the secrets of the heavens.[24]

Shaw is, therefore, quite right in representing Newton as a believer in alchemy.

Shaw's Newton is a believer in Revelation and is preoccupied with the study of the Scriptures. Charles is about to go leaving 'Mr. Newton to his mathematics'. To this Newton says:

I must correct that misunderstanding, Sir. I would not have you believe that I could be so inhospitable as to drive away my guests merely to indulge in the trifling pursuit of mathematical calculation, which leads finally nowhere. But I have more serious business in hand this morning. I am engaged in a study of the prophecies in the book of Daniel (He indicates the Bible). It may prove of the greatest importance to the world.

Newton's profound religious conception and his deep faith in God find clear expression in his reply to the artist Kneller who contemptuously says that to the scientist 'the universe is merely but a clock':

Shall I tell you a secret, Mr. Beautymonger? The clock does not keep time. If it did there would be no further need for Clockmaker. He is wiser than to leave us to our foolish selves in that fashion. When He made a confusion of tongues to prevent the Tower of Babel from reaching to heaven He also contrived a confusion of time to prevent us from doing wholly without Him. The sidereal clock, the clock of the universe, goes wrong. He has to corrcct it from time to time... But I do not know what is amiss with it. Not until the world finds this out can it do without the Clockmaker in the heavens who can set the hands back or forward, and move the stars with a touch of His almighty finger as He watches over us in the heavens.

Shaw is right in attributing to Newton this belief in the divine origin and divine governance of the universe. Newton was deeply interested in theology and his theological works *The Observations on the Prophecies of Daniel and the Apocalypse of St. John, Historical Account of Two Notable Corruptions of Scripture* are quite interesting. David Brewster says, 'The history of the theological studies of Sir Isaac Newton will ever be regarded as one of the most interesting portions of his life.'[25] Newton was a firm believer in the great doctrines of religion, and he thought that the prophecies of the Old and New Testament 'afford convincing arguments that the world is governed by Providence'.[26]

VI

Summing up, we may say that Shaw has given a correct account of Newton's belief in the possibility of the transmutation of base metals into gold, in the elixir of life, in the philosopher's stone, his religious conceptions, his faith in Revelation and God and his scriptural and theological preoccupations. But in other respects he has taken liberty with the facts of Newton's life. Pride, vanity, irritability and arrogance have been falsely attributed to him. And the chronology of the events of his life has been turned topsyturvy. Shaw's sketch of Newton is a masterpiece of anachronism. But he is 'a stage astronomer: that is an astronomer not for an age but for all time'. In a historical play facts do not matter if the general picture of the man is correct. It does not trouble anybody that Newton cannot have met Charles, Kneller and Fox and talked as he does in the play.

As regards Charles, in attributing to him impecuniosity, fondness for spaniels, laziness and capacity for hard work on occasions, interest in science, faith in the prerogatives of the King, Shaw has been quite faithful to history. His portraiture of Charles as a realist with great political sagacity, looking at everything from the point of view of expediency, and indulging in duplicity, subterfuge and equivocation, and thus ruling over England when she was seething with the turmoil of political, religious and personal quarrels is also true to history. But in some respects Shaw has taken outrageous liberty with history. His representation of Louise de Keroualle as an agent of Charles for sponging on King Luois XIV, while she was really the French King's spy on the English, is a serious distortion of a historical fact. The representation of the relations between Charles and Catherine as a model of mutual love and devotion is a perversion of a fact. Charles's view on education, the choice of rulers, the English race and conscience are the views of Shaw, and their infusion into Charles further distorts an otherwise distorted historical figure. And the conversation of Charles with his brother James and his wife Catherine contains more imagination than history. In short, Shaw's Charles is partly the Charles of history and partly a creation of Shaw.

But these distortions and contradictions do not matter, because in spite of them Shaw has succeeded in giving a clear picture of the political and religious movements that burst forth into a sudden blaze, the plots and counterplots that brewed up, the suspicion and jealousy that bedevilled the relation between the monarch and the parliament, and the other forces that made the Restoration period what it was. Instead of catching Charles in the centre of the dynamic and meaningful system of the period, influencing and being influenced by it, Shaw makes him spend most of his time with Newton, Kneller and George Fox discussing science, art, religion, and statecraft, and yet he gives a picture of the age that is quite sound. His play is based on 'what might have happened to him [Charles] but did not'. And for the occurrence of the incidents in the play he 'cannot produce a scrap of evidence, being quite convinced that they never occurred'.[27] Shaw abandons external veracity for the sake of revealing the essential truth about Charles the man, his politics, his domesticity, and above all, the age he lived in. Thus in *Good King Charles* Shaw attempts a new genre : A true history that never happened.

Notes

1. *Shaw*, p. 97.
2. Preface, pp. 153–4.
3. *Everybody's Political What's What*, p. 181.
4. *The Political History of England*, vol. VIII, pp. 11–12.
5. *Encyclopaedia Britannica*.
6. Richard Lodge, op. cit., vol. VIII, p. 90.
7. *England Under the Stuarts*, p. 291.
8. *A Short History of the English People*, p. 631.
9. Ibid., p. 631.
10. *England Under the Stuarts*, p. 314.
11. Richard Lodge, op. cit., vol. VIII, p. 106.
12. *Encyclopaedia Britannica*.
13. Richard Lodge, op. cit., vol. VIII, p. 106.
14. *England Under the Stuarts*, p. 292.
15. *Bernard Shaw; His Life, Work and Friends*, pp. 569–70.
16. *History of England*, p. 410.
17. *The Life of Sir Isaac Newton*, p. 338.
18. *G.B.S.* 90, p. 107.
19. David Brewster, *The Life of Sir Isaac Newton*, p. 338.
20. Ibid., p. 337.
21. Ibid., p. 338.
22. Ibid., p. 338.
23. Ibid., p. 302.
24. S. Winsten, *G.B.S.* 90, p. 107.
25. *The Life of Sir Isaac Newton*, p. 269.
26. Ibid., p. 280.
27. *Everybody's Political What's What*, p. 181.

Bibliography

I
Works by Bernard Shaw

Standard Edition of the Works of Bernard Shaw, Constable and Company Ltd. London.

Advice to a Young Critic, Letters, 1894–1928, Peter Owen Ltd, London, 1963.

Ellen Terry and Bernard Shaw: A Correspondence, edited by St. John Christopher, Constable and Co., London, 1931.

What I Really Wrote about the War, Constable and Co., 1931.

Shaw on Theatre, edited by E.J. West, Hill and Wang, New York, 1968.

Shaw on Shakespeare, edited and with an introduction by Edwin Wilson, Cassell, London, 1962.

W.B. Yeats—Letters to Florence Farr, edited by Clifford Bax, Home and Van Thal Ltd., London, 1946.

The Matter with Ireland, edited and with an introduction by David H.Greene and Dan H. Lawrence, Rupert Hart-Davis, London, 1962.

II
Books on Bernard Shaw

Bentley, Eric, *Bernard Shaw*, Robert Hale Ltd., London, 1950.

Chesterton, G. K., *George Bernard Shaw*, The Bodley Head, London, 1950.

Colbourne, Maurice, *The Real Bernard Shaw*, J.M. Dent and Sons Ltd., London, 1949.

Duffin, Henry Charles, *The Quintessence of Bernard Shaw*, Allen and Unwin Ltd., London, 1920.

Ervine, St. John, *Bernard Shaw: His Life, Work and Friends*, Constable and Co. Ltd., 1956.

Harris, Frank, *Bernard Shaw*, Victor Gollancz Ltd., London., 1931.

Henderson, Archibald, *Bernard Shaw: Playboy And Prophet*, D. Appleton and Co., New York, 1932.

————*George Bernard Shaw: The Man of the Century*, Appleton Century Crofts, Inc., New York, 1956.

Joad, C.E.M., *Shaw*, Victor Gallancz Ltd., London, 1949.

————*Shaw and Society: An Anthology and a Symposium*, Odhams Press, London.

Kaufmann, R. J., *G.B. Shaw—A Collection of Critical Essays*, Prentice-Hall, Inc. Englewood Cliffs, New Jersey, 1965.

Langher, Lawrence *G.B.S. and the Lunatic*, Hutchinson, London, 1964.

MacCarthy, Desmond, *Shaw*, Macgibbon and Kee, London, 1951.

Meisel, Martin, *Shaw and the Nineteenth Century Theatre*, Princeton, New Jersy, 1963.

Nethercot, Arthur H., *Man and Superman: The Shavian Portrait Gallery*, Harvard University Press, Cambridge, Massachusetts, 1954.

Patch, Blanche, *Thirty Years with G.B.S.*, Victor Gollancz Ltd., London, 1951.

Pearson, Hesketh, *G.B.S.: A Full-lenght Portrait*, Garden City, New York, 1946.

————*G.B.S.—A Postscript*, Collins, London, 1951.

Purdom, C.B,, *A Guide to the Plays of Bernard Shaw*, Methuen, London, 1964.

Robertson, J.M., *Mr. Shaw and the Maid*, Richard Cobden—Sanderson, London.

Roy, R.N., *George Bernard Shaw's Philosophy of Life*, Firma K.L. Mukhopadhyaya, Calcutta, 1964.

Sen Gupta, S. C., *The Art of Bernard Shaw*, A. Mukherjee and Co., Calcutta, second revised edition, 1950.

E. Strauss, *George Bernard Shaw*, Longmans, Green and Co., London, 1950.

Ward, A.C., *Bernard Shaw*, Longmans, Green and Co. London, 1950.

Watson, Barbara Bellow, *A Shavian Guide to the Intelligent Woman*, Chatto and Windus, London, 1964.

West, Alick, *A Good Man Fallen among Fabians*, Lawrence and Wishard Ltd., London, 1949.

Whitehead, George, *Bernard Shaw Explained*, Watts and Co., London.

Winsten, S., *G.B.S.* 90, Hutchinson, London, 1946.

————*Days with Bernard Shaw*, Hutchinson, London.

III
Books on History

Carr, E.H., *What is History*, Macmillan, London, 1962.

Collingwood, R.G., *The Idea of History*, Oxford University Press, London, 1951.

Danto, Arthur C., *Analytical Philosophy of History*, Cambridge University Press, 1966.

Finger, Ben, *Concise World History*, Peter Owen, London, 1960.

Gallie, W. B., *Philosophy and the Historical Understanding*, Chatto and Windus, London, 1964.

Gustavson, Carl G. *A Preface to History*, McGraw-Hill, London, 1955.

Renier, G.J., *History—Its Purpose and Method*, George Allen and Unwin, London, 1950.

Rickman, H. P. (ed), *Meaning in History — William Dilthey's Thoughts on History and Society*, Allen and Unwin, London 1961.

Walsh, W.H., *Philosophy of History—An Introduction*, Harper and Row, New York, and Evanston, 1966.

Widagery, Alban G., *Interpretations of History, Confucius to Toynbee*, Allen and Unwin, London, 1961.

IV
On Napoleon

Belloc, Hilaire, *Napoleon*, Cassell and Co, London, 1934.

Constant, *Recollections of the Private Life of Napoleon*, translated by Walter Clark, Saalfield, Ohio, second edition, 1904.

Ferguson, Wallace K., and Bruun, Geoffrey, *A Survey of European Civilization. Since 1500*, Houghton Mifflin, The Riverside Press, Cambridge, Massachusetts, 1958.

Ludwig, Emil, *Napoleon*, translated by Eden and Cedar Paul, Allen and Unwin, London.

Markham, Felix, *Napoleon*, Weidenfeld and Nicolson, London, 1964.

Rose J.H., *The Life of Napoleon*, tenth edition, G. Bell and Sons Ltd., London, 1929.

————*The Personality of Napoleon*, G. Bell and Sons Ltd., London, 1929.

Wheeler, F.B., *The Story of Napoleon*, George G. Harrap and Co., London.

V
On Julius Caesar

Durant, Will, *The Story of Civilization*, Part III, Simon and Schuster, New York, 1944.

Fowler, W. Warde, *Julius Caesar*, G.P. Putnam Sons, London, 1928.

Gelzer, Matthias, *Caesar—Politician and Statesman*, translated by Peter Needham, Basil Blackwell, Oxford, 1968.

Heitland, W.E., *A Short History of the Roman Republic*, Cambridge University Press, London, 1929.

Liddell, Henry G., *History of Rome*, John Murray, London, 1879.

Ludwig, Emil, *Cleopatra, the Story of a Queen*, translated by Bernard Miall, Bantam Books, New York, 1938.

Mommsen, Theodor, *The History of Rome*, translated by William Purdie Dickson, vol. V, Macmillan, London, 1931.

Plutarch, *Lives*, translated by John and William Langhorne, Walter Scott Ltd., London.

Suetonius, Tranquillus Gaius, *The Twelve Caesars*, translated by Robert Graves, Penguin Books, 1958.

VI
On Saint Joan

Barrett, W.B., *The Trial of Jeanne d'Arc.*, English translation, George Routledge, Kegan Paul, Trench Trubner and Co., London, 1931.

Bernanos, Georges, *Sanity Will Out*, translated by R. Bachelor, Sheet and and Ward, New York, 1947.

Coulton, G.G., *Inquisition and Liberty*, William Heinemann, London, 1938.

Denis, Leon, *The Mystery of Joan of Arc,* translated by Arthur Conan Doyle, John Murray, London, 1924.

Fabre, Lucian, *Joan of Arc*, translated by Gerard Hopkins, Odhams Press Ltd., London, 1954.

France, Anatole, *The Life of Joan of Arc*, translated by Winifred Stephens, in three vols., John Lane, The Bodley Head, Ltd., London, 1909.

Gower, Lord Ronald, *Joan of Arc*, John C. Nimmo, London.

Lang, Andrew, *The Maid of France*, Longmans, Green and Co., London, 1929.

Lightbody, Charles Wayland, *The Judgments of Joan*, Longmans, Green and Co., London, 1929.

Murray, T. Duglas, *Jeanne d' Arc*, McClare, Phillips and Co., New York, 1902.

Paine, Albert Bidelow, *The Girl in White Armour*, Macmillan, New York, 1927.

Pernoud, Regine, *The Retrial of Joan of Arc*, translated by J. M. Cohen, Methuen, London, 1955.

Scott, W.S., *The Trial of Joan*, The Folio Society, London, 1956.

Sackville-West, Victoria, *Saint Joan of Arc*, Cobden-Sanderson, London, 1936.

Twain, Mark, *Personal Recollections of Joan of Arc*, translated by Winifred Stephens, The Bodley Head, London, 1909.

Waldman, Milton, *Joan of Arc*, Little Brown and Co., Boston, 1975.

VII

On Charles II

Brewster, David, *The Life of Sir Isaac Newton*, John Murray, 1831.

Clark, G.N., *The Later Stuarts*, 1660–1714, Oxford University Press, 1934.

Green, John Richard, *A Short History of the English People*, Macmillan, London, 1952.

Leonard, Philipp, *A History of Scientific Progress*, G. Bell and Sons, London, 1933.

Lockyer, Roger and Smith, David, *A History of England*, English Language Book Society and Ernest Benn Ltd.

Lodge, Richard, *The Political History of England*, vol. VIII, 1606–1702, Longmans, Green and Co., London, 1923.

Macaulay, T.B., The History of England, vol. I, fifth editon, Longmans, Brown, Green and Longmans, London, 1849.

Trevelyan, G.M., *England under the Staurts*, Methuen, London, 1954.

VIII

On Biology

Barnett, S.A. (ed), *A Century of Darwin*, William Heinemann, London, 1959.

Bergson, Henri, *Creative Evolution*, translated by Arthur Mitchell, The Modern Library, New York, 1964.

————*Matter and Memory*, translated by Nancy Margaret Paul and Walter Scott Palmer, Allen and Unwin, London, 1919.

————*Time and Free-Will*, translated by F.L. Pogson, Allen and Unwin, London, 1950.

Butler, Samuel, *Evolution Old and New*, edited by R.A. Stratfield, A.C. Fifield, London, 1911.

————*Life and Habit*, second edition, Trubner and Co., London, 1878.

————*Luck or Cunning*, Trubner and Co., London, 1887.

————*Unconscious Memory*, new edition, A.C. Fifield, London, 1910.

Darwin, Charles, *The Origin of Species*, sixth edition, Oxford University Press, London, 1961.

Hardy, A.C., and Ford, E.B., (eds), *Evolution as a Process*, Allen and Unwin Ltd., London, 1964.

Huxley, Julian, *Evolution in Action*, A Mentor Book, the New American Library, 1953.

Huxley, Thomas Henry, and Huxley, Julian, *Evolution and Ethics*, 1893-1943, The Pilot Press Ltd, London.

Keith, Sir Arthur, *Essays on Human Evolution*, Watts and Co, London, 1947.

Lamarck, Jean-Baptiste, *Zoological Philosophy*, translated by Hugh Elliott, Macmillan, London, 1914.

Shull, A Franklin, *Evolution*, McGraw-Hill, New York, 1951.

Simpson, George Gaylord, *The Meaning of Evolution*, A Mentor Book, The New American Library, 1948.

Wells, H.G., Huxley, Julian, and Wells, G.P., *The Science of Life*, Cassell and Co., London, 1931.

IX
Miscellaneous Books

Bentley, Eric, *The Cult of the Superman*, Robert Hale Ltd., London, 1947.

Bogard, Tour and Oliver, William, *Modern Drama*, Oxford University Press, New York, 1965.

Bradbook, M.C., *Ibsen the Norwegian*, Chatto and Windus, London, 1948.

Berlin, Isaiah, *Karl Marx—His Life and Environment*, Oxford University Press, London, 1951.

Bullough, Geoffrey, *Narrative and Dramatic Sources of Shakespeare*, vols. III and IV, Routledge and Kegan Paul, London, 1962.

Cole, Toby, *Playwrights on Playwriting*, Hill and Wang, New York, 1960.

Collins, A.S., *English Literature of the Twentieth Century*, University Tutorial Press, London, 1951.

Daiches, David, *A Critical History of English Literature*, vol. II, Secker and Warburg, London, 1960.

Durant, Will, *The Story of Philosophy*, Garden City, New York, 1933.

Egerton, Hugh Edward, *A Short History of British Colonial Policy*, 1606-1909, Methuen, London, 1950.

Gray, Alexander, *The Socialist Tradition—Moses to Lenin*, Longmans, Green and Co., London, 1948.

Ibsen, Henrik, *Eleven Plays of Henrik Ibsen*, The Modern Library, New York.

Joad, C.E.M, *Matter, Life and Value*, Oxford University Press, London, 1929.

Macardle, Dorothy, *The Irish Republic*, Victor Gollancz, London, 1937.

Mann, Thomas, *The Living Thoughts of Schopenhauer*, Cassell and Co., London, 1942.

Marx, Karl, *Das Kapital*.

———A critique of Political Economy, Translated from the fourth German Edition by Eden and Cedar Paul, George Allen and Unwin Ltd., London, 1929.

Nicoll, Allardyce, *The Theory of Drama*, George G. Harrap and Co. Ltd., London, 1937.

——*British Drama*, George G. Harrap and Co. Ltd., London, 1962.

English Drama: *A Modern Viewpoint*, George G. Harrap and Co. Ltd. London, 1968.

——*A History of English Drama*, *Vol. V*, Cambridge At the University Press, 1959.

Plato, *The Republic*, Translated by Benjamin Jowett, The World Publishing Co., Cleveland and New York, 1946.

Russell, Bertrand, *An Outline af Philosophy*, George Allen and Unwin Ltd., London, 1932.

Schopenhauer, Arthur, *The Work of Schopenhauer*, Abridged, Edited by Will Durant, Garden City Publishing Co., Inc., New York, 1928.

Sen Gupta, S.C., *Shakespeare's Historical Plays*, Oxford University Press, 1964.

Tillyard, E.M.W., *Shakespeare's Historical Plays*, Chatto and Windus, London, 1959.

Trevelyan, G.M., *English Social History*, Longman, Green and Co. Ltd., London, 1948.

——History of England, Longman, Green & Co. Ltd., London, 1945.

Wells, H.G., *The Outline of History,* Cassell & Co., London, 1956.

Williams, Raymond, *Drama From Ibsen to Eliot*, Penguin Books, Inc. Association with Chatto & Windus, London, 1964.

Index